Psycho-Energetics

If today isn't all you'd like it to be,
if tomorrow holds no promise of change

Psycho-Energetics

Remember that a lifestyle learned,
is a lifestyle lived

Psycho-Energetics

When your present is past,
and your future is today

Use psycho-energetics—today's way to a new you!

Psycho-Energetics
by Dr. Paul Mok

PINNACLE BOOKS • LOS ANGELES

For CASK—
    Love, love, and more love

PSYCHO-ENERGETICS

Copyright © 1972 by Dr. Paul Mok

An original Pinnacle Books edition, originally published under the title RECYCLE YOUR LIFESTYLE, published for the first time anywhere.

ISBN: 0-523-40321-7

First printing, November, 1972
Second printing, March 1978

Printed in the United States of America

PINNACLE BOOKS
One Century Plaza
2029 Century Park East
Los Angeles, California 90067

CONTENTS

Preface   7

PART ONE   PSYCHO-ENERGETICS FOR SELF-MASTERY   9

1. Thinking of Yourself as an Energy System   11
2. How to Resist and Control Negative Forces   25
3. Roadmaps to the Now and the New   69
4. Are You Ready for an Exciting Lift-off?   84
5. Strengthening Attitudes, Eliminating Bad Habits   91

PART TWO   PSYCHO-ENERGETICS FOR BETTER RELATIONSHIPS   113

6. Are You in Touch . . . Do You Relate to Yourself?   115
7. Interacting, a Technique for Success   133
8. Self-Suggestion—Action—Satisfaction   156
9. Recharging Your Psychic Energy System   171
10. Communicating More Effectively—With Anyone   188

PART THREE   PSYCHO-ENERGETICS FOR AN INTEGRATED ACTION PATTERN THAT WORKS FOR YOU!   199

11. Getting It Together—For You   201
12. The Necessity of Change Without Damage   212
13. Recycling as a Positive Way of Life   222

Preface

Since the original printing of *Psycho-Energetics,* a tremendous amount has happened to me. Most important, I have used the techniques described in the book to do these things:

1. Enrich my life.
2. Do things I would not have dared before.
3. Relax and learn to enjoy it.
4. Open up new interests.
5. Develop new and lasting friendships.
6. Start a new business.
7. Actualize my dreams instead of dreaming life away.

Some of the practical results of using psycho-energetics in my own daily life have included breaking away from the humdrum hassle of commuting; designing seminars that have helped hundreds of business people increase their personal mastery of challenging and difficult daily stress situations; traveling across the nation and around the world to give speeches and conduct workshops for people like you anxious to grow and enjoy better lives right now. Today!

If, after you have read *Psycho-Energetics,* you would like to obtain more information about me, my qualifications as a speaker/seminar-leader, my customized

workshops—"Victory Thru Situational Mastery";
"Management Behavior and Self-Directed Change";
"Relationship-Selling"; "Effective Time Management"; "Conference and Meeting Leadership"; or
"Communicating Styles"—or if you would like to
obtain, at no cost, information about my videotapes,
audio-cassette programs, self-study communication
materials—please drop me a line:

> Paul Mok
> PMA Professional Building
> 4519 W. Lovers Lane
> Dallas, Texas 75209

You may call me, my wife, Vi, or my colleagues at
(214) 357-0487. It will be a genuine pleasure hearing from you.

Meanwhile, enjoy applying psycho-energetics and
discover the exciting, adventurous, action individual
you always wanted to be and doubted you might become. As you believe and act, so you will be; and
believe me, it *is* a great and joyous experience when
you begin living your dream!

> Paul Mok
> Dallas, Texas
> September 1977

PART ONE

PSYCHO-ENERGETICS FOR

SELF-MASTERY

1. THINKING OF YOURSELF AS AN ENERGY SYSTEM

How to Plan and Organize Your Energy Investments

Have You Thought About Yourself as a Human Energy Mechanism?

All of us are seeking to improve our lifestyles. In recent months, lifestyle has become a number one topic of conversation. Go to a cocktail party, eavesdrop on the bus, speak with a group of teenagers—and bang!—there it is: lifestyle, lifestyle, lifestyle.

The word has assumed a fashionable mystique. Every popular magazine you pick up these days has an article, a new slant, a research report, an alleged first-person documentary exposé on lifestyle. But when all is said and done, most of the popular writers have missed the point—lifestyle is not a place, it is not a new environment, it is not something you find outside of yourself, it is *decidedly* not a cop-out fantasy rainbow to moon about, to call your travel agent about. Lifestyle does not involve joining a vacation club, flying now and paying later for a sojourn on a Caribbean island; nor does it mean that you should abandon your family and join a commune; nor does it require escaping to some Waldenesque, rural cabin retreat.

Let's face it. If you make the assumption, even for a moment, that lifestyle change is something that happens to you from outside or is done to you, you are going to miss the point, and chances are you never will be able to effect a basically new and more fulfilling pattern of living.

Forget everything you've heard about lifestyle up until today! Forget those articles and picture magazine versions of fun in the sun! Forget everything you've heard at cocktail parties. None of those things really counts!

What *does* count is YOU! Your needs. Your fears and worries. Your desires and aspirations. Your energy—and what you do with it. This is what it's all about. Other people would like to trick you into forgetting this basic fact, namely that lifestyle begins with you. They'd like to con you into thinking an improved lifestyle is something you get or something you buy, because if they can make you believe that, they can sell you something: fancy food, health farms, vacations, you name it.

Frankly, I think you're a bit too smart and too skeptical for this updated, snake-oil approach. But still all of us in America are looking for shortcuts. We want instant remedies for our ills; we'd like to begin that romantic new lifestyle tomorrow! But realistically speaking, anything worth having is worth an expenditure of time and effort.

Here are some guidelines which will make it possible for you to get started on the less romantic, but infinitely more fulfilling and realistic road to increased personal effectiveness and satisfaction:

1. Don't try to imitate anyone else's lifestyle. Remember: you've got to work out a new pattern of living that's right, that's tailored for you and you alone!
2. Make haste slowly! If you go off half-cocked or try to follow superficial formulas, you'll only get superficial results!

3. Rome wasn't built in a day. Developing a new, meaningful and realistic lifestyle takes time, rigorous thinking, introspection, planning, step-by-step experimentation. It's a slow but nevertheless exciting adventure.

4. Avoid the New Year's resolutions approach! Good intentions are fine, but what are they really? *Intentions,* that's all! If lifestyle does not involve changed behavior, it isn't a lifestyle change. Remember that! It's very easy to con yourself into thinking that a new intention represents a meaningful change. As you proceed through this practical and personal manual for recycling your own life style, ask yourself every several days, "What have I really done today that was different from my old action pattern?"

5. Gear your thinking and actions to short-term results! You can't walk to California in one giant step. By the same token, if you think about lifestyle change as a melodramatic one hundred and eighty degree turn in the road, you'll fall on your face!

6. Practice modesty even when you succeed and are tempted to tell the world about the new you! Bragging about what you are doing will only cause those who love you most to distrust what you are trying to do. They'll expect too much of you too soon. Worse, you'll wind up expecting too much of yourself. If you fail to deliver on your own pronouncements, you'll get discouraged and give up. Avoid that pitfall from the start. Savor the private excitement and joy of doing things differently. Let your new action pattern speak for itself!

7. Start keeping a lifestyle diary! Before this week is over, spend about sixty cents and buy yourself a

spiral notebook. Divide it into three sections as follows: Section One, *Lifestyle is Me!;* Section Two, *Lifestyle is Interacting More Effectively with Others!;* Section Three, *Lifestyle Is Action—My Actions.* In the pages ahead, you will learn, step by step, how to use your diary: how to inventory your strengths and weaknesses; how to pinpoint what parts of your self-image need to be improved. And you'll learn lots of ways to use the diary as a means of checking on yourself and of testing how real and how significant your attempts at recycling your lifestyle really are.

The single most distinguishing difference between living beings and inanimate objects is—energy! A living human being, and that means *you,* is nothing more nor less than a walking, breathing, feeling, acting and reacting mechanism of energy. Whether your lifestyle is effective or self-defeating depends above all on how you use your basic energy potential!

Let me give you an example. Stop and think for a moment about all the things you did yesterday. Were you happy? Did you waste time? Did you spin your wheels? Were you worrying a lot? Did you find yourself daydreaming? Did you find yourself getting exasperated at others? Did you sigh and perhaps feel bogged down at times? If you are a normal, typical American, the answers to these questions almost inevitably are "yes." But how necessary was all that discouragement, all that worry, all that wheel-spinning and all that frustration?

I'm going to prove to you in the course of this book that probably more than eighty per cent of the frustration you experience on any given day of your life could

14

have been prevented! That's right, I know it's hard to believe, but it's true. Let me tell you why.

The single most important reason why human beings become frustrated and upset is because they've given up before they even start. More specifically, it's because we *squander* our energy instead of *investing it!*

Let's take the typical thirty-year-old American male and illustrate exactly what's likely to occur on a given frustrating day of his life. No sooner does he wake up in the morning than he starts worrying. Instead of calmly thinking that everything he feels and thinks and does this day is going to reflect his lifestyle—or the lack of it—instead of calmly, objectively and positively planning how he is going to invest his energy and time for maximum satisfaction and effectiveness, he merely allows diffuse psychic energy to go where it will; to control him. He starts worrying about his job. While he's shaving, he's already brooding about things that may have happened yesterday or the day before. Without realizing it, he's beginning the day on a defensive, defeatist note. His children are making noise now as they get ready for school. He allows these normal everyday behaviors to upset him. Because he is already starting to look out the window of the new day through a negative screen, he's likely to be more bothered by the sing-song behavior of his children than pleased at their natural exuberance. He snaps at them or his wife, making whoever is nearest his whipping boy. His crankiness immediately sets into motion a cycle of counter-reacting crankiness. When his wife or children react negatively to his bad mood, he becomes disgusted with them. Now, in addition to worrying about what happened yesterday and what's likely to occur today, he unwittingly begins investing valuable human energy in needless resentment.

Only thirty minutes of the new day have unfolded,

and already he has squandered eighteen hundred seconds of vital and creative human energy! Not only that, without realizing it and certainly without wanting to, he has set the stage for wasting more energy throughout the day. He has triggered a self-destructive mechanism of cyclical, negative chain reactions. He will leave the house in a bad mood, preoccupied with the frustrations and resentments of his first unsatisfactory waking hour, and if he is like most of us, he will then start blaming himself for being such a louse. On his way to work he will soon find himself bogged down in his daily pattern of self-recrimination and guilt. *Why did I holler at the kids? Why did I take out my frustrations on my wife? What's the matter with me anyway?* The next forty-five minutes to an hour will thus become a wheel-spinning, unproductive playback of self-torment.

And so his day goes. From needless unproductive worry, to needless unproductive frustration, to needless and unproductive resentment, to needless and unproductive self-accusations—he'll be lucky if he can break out of this destructive, seemingly endless cycle for one golden half-hour. More likely than not, as he kicks off his shoes that night, he'll be completely exhausted and limp as a result of his colossal yet completely unintentional misapplication of his own vital human energy!

If You Don't Direct Your Energies, Your Energies Will Direct You!

Needless to say, the frustrated fellow we were just talking about did not direct his energies. Clearly, they directed him. It's easy to see it happening with someone else, isn't it? But let's be absolutely honest. Doesn't the same thing happen to you? Hasn't the process been an almost everyday occurrence? Be honest now. If it hasn't, you needn't read any further. But if it has, you must honestly face up to the fact that you have been squandering your energy instead of directing it and making it work for you. You are then ready to really begin thinking about a new lifestyle.

I said earlier that there is no mystique about lifestyle It is nothing more than your everyday pattern of living! Lifestyle is the sum total of what you are, what you think you are, how you see other people, how they see you, what you desire to become, and what you are doing about it on an everyday basis!

Why have I titled this self-help manual, *Psycho-Energetics?* The answer is quite simple. It is only by *redirecting* your presently wasted, squandered, unproductive energy that you can achieve a new and more fulfilling lifestyle! Yes, it's true, there is no way to get around it. I know there are many of us, plenty of close friends of mine and yours too, I imagine, who would like to go on living exactly as they are and achieve an improved, satisfying, new lifestyle in the bargain. Forget it. It's an infantile blue bubble. A fantasy that isn't going to happen.

Do you realize how much vital human energy and how much vital energy potential you waste every day? Probably not. That's part of the problem. If you haven't really thought about this and have never taken the time or trouble to calculate how much energy you've wasted, you'll never know. But it's time that you did.

Suppose you never stopped and figured how you were spending your weekly salary. Suppose you never used a budget? Would you be able to pay your bills on time? Would you be able to have savings left over in the bank? Certainly not. In order to achieve economic stability, independence and prosperity, it is absolutely essential that you come to grips with ways that you've been squandering your money, analyze specific mistakes, develop a new and realistic plan and stick to it.

We've all heard the cliché "money isn't everything, happiness is more important." I believe that's true. But I also believe that the only way to happiness is to invest, direct, channel and control your self-energy in exactly the same way you do with your financial resources.

Next week, after you've purchased the notebook mentioned earlier, I'm going to ask you to do something very basic and very necessary—inventory your energy expenditures every day for one solid week! It's going to be difficult, and it may seem annoying, but bear with me. Taking that inventory may be the biggest leap you've ever made toward achieving what up until now has been the elusive dream of a really fulfilling new lifestyle!

What is Your Self-Image Screen?

You've probably heard of the term *self-image*. Very simply, what this means is how you think about yourself. In other words you may have the image of yourself as a has-been, a person who is trying to cling to life and avoid being hurt by other people. You may have the image of yourself as a basically decent person, a good husband and father, a guy who just wants to live and let live. Maybe your self-image is that of a potentially great person, a talented and imaginative individual who will someday, somehow, achieve some great breakthrough which will cause the world to take note and shower you with acclaim.

But how useful are such self-images? Not very, I'm afraid. Obviously, they are too general, too amorphous to provide any real use to those of us who may have thought of ourselves along these lines.

Seriously and objectively, you must realize that you have not merely one self-image but many—and that all of them are operating simultaneously. For example, a person might see himself as an effective socializer and a good friend to others, an average breadwinner, an outstanding father and a somewhat erratic husband! All of these separate self-images may be validly based upon things that he has done or is doing and feedback he's received. But recognizing this—the many faces we wear to different people and accepting such reality— does not necessarily provide any helpful insight for designing a new and improved life style. Quite to the contrary, most of us are inclined to use these separate self-images as justifications for going on behaving the way we've behaved before.

What's missing in the separate self-image approach toward understanding human behavior is what I call the *screen concept*. Every one of us wants to be secure within himself. But beyond economic safety and well-being, where does this security come from? It comes from the knowledge of our own self-predictability. In other words if you can automatically assume that on most week days you'll be working for eight hours, that you'll eat three meals a day, that you'll spend some time at home after work relaxing—reading, watching television or socializing with family and friends—you can approach each new day with a certain sense of security, albeit perhaps without excitement.

Several basic factors contribute to this self-consistency. The first is habit—your conditioned pattern of behavior. You tend to unconsciously model Wednesday's actions on Tuesday's actions, 1973's actions on 1972's, and so forth. But self-consistency extends beyond the force of mere habit and past conditioning. Without knowing it perhaps, and without thinking about it in a rigorous way before now, your daily actions have represented in fact certain underlying assumptions that you have about yourself. You may have assumed, for example, that you are a pretty average person—reasonably bright but no Einstein genius, average in energy but no human dynamo, a basically cooperative person who would like others to think well of him and who therefore tries in countless little ways each day to be considerate and accommodating. What do these self-assumptions add up to? *A self-attitudinal screen!*

The self-attitudinal screen of the kind of person I've just described is basically a defensive one. Think about it for a minute. The individual who thinks he isn't really very bright is likely to let others speak first and to follow their lead. Why not? He doesn't want to risk making a fool of himself; it's easier and safer to let others babble and then react. A person who thinks of himself as being not particularly energetic is certainly not likely to take unusual initiative or dramatic action. Again, he will more likely perform those activities which others expect of him and which do not involve either a high risk or a high potential of exhilaration or adventure. A person who likes to think of himself as being a good guy will probably go out of his way in countless little ways each day when he shouldn't, because again he seeks to preserve the consistency, the predictability, the stability of his good-guyism. Thus, the defensive's self-attitudinal screen shapes his behavior without his realizing it.

What Is My Own Basic Self-Attiudinal Screen?

Here is a simple and effective way for beginning to zero in on your own basic self-attitudinal screen. Think for a moment about two of your best points. Two fundamental, outstanding characteristics which others have frequently complimented you on. No wishful thinking now. This has to be absolutely candid and based on real feedback, nothing else. On a piece of scratch paper write down these two most complimented characteristics—those two aspects about your own character which you know are good. Now comes the tricky part. Take two or three minutes and consider this question: If I did these two things to the extreme, what main problem would I be likely to encounter?

Let me give you an example. Suppose an individual listed his two main strengths as honesty and having the courage of his convictions. Fine. Now suppose that he carried these two characteristics to the extreme—what problems might he encounter? That's right—outspokenness and stubbornness. While he has always thought positively of himself as being a very honest person, chances are that he is, in actuality, overly outspoken. When others get in his way, he'll complain too fast, find fault unnecessarily, jump to conclusions perhaps, and irritate those around him by being unnecessarily critical.

Suppose you wrote down that one of your main strengths was a quality of decisiveness. Fine. But suppose you are overly decisive, decisive to a fault. What problem would you encounter? That's right. You'd tend to oversimplify things. You'd make decisions too quickly—on the basis of too little data and too little reflection. Your invisible self-attitudinal screen would be covering up impatience—impulsivity. Thus, when things happened that began to frustrate and irritate you, your self-attitudinal screen would swing into action and bang! You'd immediately commit yourself to a given course of action—nothing indecisive or ambiguous about you! No, sir!

Now, I think you have the idea. It was Alexander Dumas who said that any virtue carried to the extreme

21

becomes a crime. Therefore, we're likely to discover our basic hangups or stumbling blocks not by looking outside at those people or events that get in our way, but rather, by taking our virtues, or our "plus" characteristics, and mentally exaggerating them into the spectrum of weakness.

Take fairness, for example. If a person bent over backwards to be fair, he'd become indecisive! In some cases, when he thinks positively that he's being fair, others will secretly believe that he is being indecisive.

Take the person who thinks of himself as being imaginative and creative. If he let his imagination run away with him, how would he behave? That's right, in an undisciplined fashion! While he's congratulating himself on his ability to manufacture a dozen bright new ideas on the spur of the moment, others are secretly wondering when he is going to select one idea and follow it through to successful completion.

Reflect Before You Act—Setting the Stage to Re-energize Your Life

Plan to spend one week seriously and objectively— but not in a worrisome way—thinking about yourself and those around you before beginning the step-by-step program for recycling your lifestyle. Too many people have gone off half-cocked, embarking on programs that weren't right for them, stacking the cards against themselves without even realizing it. Don't let that happen to you!

During the next week, try to check yourself when you start worrying. Start thinking about yourself as a mechanism of human energy. Think about the kind of person you are now and the kind of person you'd gradually like to become.

22

Be self-objective, I know it's hard, but self-flattery leads to self-destruction. On the other hand, selling yourself short is equally self-destructive.

Ask yourself whether you are really willing to spend several months inventorying yourself, experimenting in a program of self-directed change. It will take time and a lot of self-discipline. I don't want you to postpone too long the launching of your own self-development program, but on the other hand, you must be careful to avoid a flash-in-the-pan spurt of enthusiasm which will quickly fade.

Look at those around you with new eyes during the next week. Don't react to them as you usually would, but observe them very carefully as mechanisms of human energy. How are they utilizing their greatest treasure? Are they directing their energies or squandering them? Are they avoiding taking new and unfamiliar paths toward self-realization in order to preserve the security that comes from screening daily experience in a defensively oriented way?

By getting out of your old subjective head and looking at those you know best in this new objective fashion, you will set the stage for being able to look at *yourself* in a rigorous and disciplined objective fashion which, of course, is much harder! But believe me, it will become infinitely rewarding!

I would suggest that you not try to rush through this book. Take it in small doses, one step at a time. Put the book to one side at the end of this chapter. Think about who you are, about what you did today, yesterday, this past week. How much self-agonizing did you do? How much of it was really necessary?

Then start looking at and analyzing those around you in the same way. If you can, take some notes on what you see, what you hear, what you think. Jotting

23

down these notes—even on the back of an envelope if necessary—will help. And don't forget to buy that spiral notebook. You'll be ready to begin using it in a few days.

2. HOW TO RESIST AND CONTROL NEGATIVE FORCES

You Must and Can Recycle Presently Wasted Energy!

What Worry Mechanisms Really Are

In the past few days I hope you have really been observing those around you; family members, colleagues at work, close friends, even strangers. What have you noticed?

You've probably noticed that other people—perhaps even people whom heretofore you were inclined to envy—were really tied up. They seemed tense. Tired. Frustrated.

Did you notice how little laughter you observed? How few people seemed to be smiling most of the time?

Did you notice the way they walked and sat? These are important behavioral clues. Most of the people one sees walking on the street do not hold their shoulders back, do not appear to be proud and optimistic. Quite to the contrary, they shuffle—almost as victims already earmarked for some mysterious and inevitable doom. What about the conversations you tuned in to? How much of the time were those closest to you complaining? Much more than *they* realized, I am sure.

Do you suppose for an instant that these individuals—many of them well educated, quite intelligent and talented—realized to what extent they were wasting, squandering their most valuable asset: ENERGY!? No, they probably didn't. I am sure we could agree that these so-called normal friends and associates made no conscious decision to shuffle down the street, to frown and sigh and complain; to feel tired and bogged down; to project an image of being frustrated, beaten down, discouraged, clinging helplessly to life. The process just happened.

But did it?

Think about it. Really think about it. Was it truly external circumstances that had beaten down these individuals? Had they lost everything? Had their homes been razed to the ground by fire? Had their loved ones been incarcerated and tortured in concentration camps? Had the death sentence of terminal illness been meted out upon them? Probably not.

More likely, they were projecting that sense of futility, of tragedy, of defeatism, of ennui, of spiritlessness which has frequently been termed the "American malaise."

Perhaps they have deceived themselves into thinking they are up against incalculable, unconquerable external negative forces. But if such is not the case—and it hardly ever is—of what are they really the victims?

That is the question. And the answer, as it will be revealed to you more and more, is that they were the victims not of *external* forces, but of *internal* forces. They, your friends and mine, have themselves created the Frankensteins that haunt them, that bear them down, that hold them in deathlike clutches, that drain and sap their vital human energy!

But what are these monstrous internal negative forces? Where do they come from? How do they work?

I call these negative forces the "Eleven Deadly Sins" of energy loss. I will enumerate them below. Then, as each is examined in turn, use your new lifestyle diary to make some self-objective notes that will show you how unwittingly you've misapplied your own vital energy resources. Read the list slowly and think carefully, if you will, about each one.

Eleven Deadly Sins of Energy Loss

1. Preoccupation with mistakes
2. Guilt
3. Anger
4. Self-blame
5. Fear
6. Self-punishment
7. Anxiety
8. Assumed failure
9. The need to possess
10. Over-reactions
11. Obsessions

All right. Let's examine them, systematically and slowly. Get your notebook now. When you have finished each section, stop reading and just reflect for a few minutes. Then list those things which you have done recently—just within the past month—which apply to the section you have just read.

1. *Preoccupation with mistakes*——Everyone makes mistakes, this is nothing new. It is inevitable because we are human and less than perfect. When you think about it, most mistakes we make can be broadly categorized under two headings. The first is: *mistakes due to impulsive or precipitant action.* That is, mistakes caused by inadequate reflection, by failing to mobilize the logic and patience of which we are all capable. Mistakes of haste. Mistakes we made because we didn't heed the good counsel of others—or our own inner objective voices.

The second category can be termed: *mistakes due*

to indecision. Mistakes of hesitation, of failing to seize a good opportunity, of failing to move when we should have. Mistakes of omission rather than of commission.

Typically, what happens when we make a mistake, one which we regard as being quite serious? Rather than rolling with the punches, as the saying goes, rather than taking our losses and reminding ourselves of the good things we've done, of the many *nonmistakes* we've made, we begin to brood. We mull over all our mistakes. We hold them up to the light, we look back on them. We ask ourselves rhetorically, time and time again, "Why did I do it?" "Why was I so stupid?" Or, "Why didn't I make the move? What was wrong with me? Why didn't I have the guts?"

And this begins a cyclical process of vital energy waste which is infinitely more serious in terms of everyday lifestyle than the original mistake we made —no matter how grave.

Now start thinking about yourself. Think back on the two or three most serious mistakes you made in the past year or two.

Perhaps you made a poor financial investment, one that has since gone sour.

Perhaps you had a golden opportunity to help a friend or perhaps even one of your own children— and you blew it.

Perhaps you were offered a rare opportunity for a new and challenging job in another area and mulled over it too long—the ship sailed and ever since you've let it haunt you: *Why didn't I make the move? What held me back?*

Perhaps you let someone talk you into something which you later regretted. In a moment of haste you agreed to pay for your ex-wife's allergy shots. Now the bills seem endless. Why did you do it?

Maybe you permitted your teenage son or daughter to go away on a trip with friends for a three- or four-day-long weekend and as soon as the youngster was out of the house you began to worry. Then perhaps before the weekend was over, you received a telephone call that your youngster had been in an automobile accident, had broken his leg or had his face cut and was now waiting to be picked up by you in some far away hospital. And immediately the torment began: *How could I have permitted the child to go? What was the matter with me? I knew I shouldn't have done it. Have I lost my reason? Perhaps God is already punishing us.* And so forth.

Now, take your diary and write down those two or three serious mistakes. Leave sufficient space, perhaps a third or half page under each mistake. Now—and this is the hard part, requiring really blunt self-honesty—try to list the number of days *just in the past month alone* when you have thought back on each serious mistake. If you don't remember exactly, make an estimate.

When I have asked business executives to perform this exercise, I have found something very interesting: most of the serious mistakes they make within the course of a year seem so grievous to them that they tend to preoccupy themselves with regrets *every day!* If that's true in your case, put down the phrase "part of each day."

Now think again. How much time on a given day would you estimate that you spent preoccupying yourself, thinking back, torturing yourself about each given mistake? Did you think about it when you woke up this morning? Did it flash back several

29

times during the day? Did you think about it again last night as you were trying to go asleep?

Again, be absolutely honest with yourself. Don't try to deny it. Don't start kidding yourself—*Oh, I didn't really think that much about it*—when you know you did. Was it twenty minutes a day? An hour? Fifteen minutes in the morning, fifteen or twenty minutes during the day? Perhaps another hour late at night? Add up the estimated subtotal of minutes when you looked back on each serious mistake during a given day and list the total time involved.

Now step back from yourself, as it were, and think about what form this self-preoccupation, this negative internal force took. Did it take the form of needless worry? Tension? Did the preoccupation with what you did wrong—or the action you should have taken but didn't—cause you to be impatient with your loved ones? Did it cause you to get a headache? Did the preoccupation interfere with your digestion? Did the amount of time you spent worrying cause you *not* to do something else that would have been fun? Did you fail to read or enjoy social conversation or perhaps do some self-renewing physical exercises because you were bogged down in the quagmire of this self-preoccupation? Also, think about the typical forms your preoccupation with mistakes usually takes.

Now stop. Write some notes. Make a list. Under the mistake and the time spent worrying about it, put down what form this self-preoccupation took. Frequently, one mistake assumes multiple forms of self-preoccupation. If you had a dialogue with yourself, write that down. Write down what you told yourself. Yes, that's right—the exact words you said to yourself late at night when you were tossing and turning and feeling like hitting your head against a wall.

After you've done that, you should honestly put down the degree to which this self-preoccupation helped you. Did it help you a little? Did it make you feel better? If so, how?

I think, if you're really being candid, you'll admit that your self-preoccupation didn't help you at all. It didn't undo the mistake, did it? If it's true, then write down "Zero—nothing—the above self-preoccupations did not help me one single bit!" Now skip several spaces and write down these words: "Things I might have done during this time (this hour-and-a-half, this forty-five minutes, whatever the amount of time spent actually was) which might have provided me with a feeling of satisfaction instead of the dissatisfaction I experienced."

The following are a few examples. Write down any that apply or appeal to you, or substitute some of your own which might be even more applicable: listening to music, taking a walk outdoors, playing with the baby, going for a run with the dog, shooting the breeze with friends, reading a good book.

See! This is where recycling your life style really begins! Now we're getting down to the nitty-gritty. As a professional psychologist, I made the mistake in earlier years of getting too bogged down, too preoccupied with technical jargon. You know what I mean—using words like *Oedipus complex, cathexis, transference, role fragmentation, identity crisis*—all that high fallutin' malarky which they taught me up at Harvard. Then, in the course of working for many years with real people, I experienced a humbling revelation: our real problems have not read psychology textbooks, our real problems in daily living have nothing to do with complexes, they have

31

to do with the daily misapplication of human energy! I began helping business men redirect their biological, social and psychic energies toward increased effectiveness, personal happiness, self-knowledge, and improved relations with other people. I call this process—the one in which you have started to participate—*psychoenergetics*.

If you have honestly performed the above exercise, it will probably represent a significant breakthrough for you toward eventually achieving a meaningful new lifestyle. You can't build a strong, sound new lifestyle on top of a negative, self-destructive foundation. First you must clean the old sludge out of your mental carburetors.

Having become aware of the tremendous amount of needless, self-defeating and fatiguing time and energy you invested just on those few serious mistakes, I think you'll be much more aware of how precious your energy really is—and less inclined to give in, from now on, to the first of these eleven deadly sins.

2. *Guilt*——We've all heard the saying, "To err is human, to forgive, divine." I believe this is essentially true, yet the real meat of this saying has gone unnoticed by most people.

Most normal, hard-working Americans with whom I have worked or been associated with socially, could be termed basically decent men and women. In general, they're not highly vindictive or relentlessly unforgiving. They're not usually angry for any length of time at their wives, children, colleagues or subordinates. By the same token, many men have frequently told me that their wives are quite forgiving when they come home late, when they have had too much to drink, when they have failed to call and say they'd be staying in town.

32

From this evidence, then, one might suppose we're already living in an era of relative forgiveness. Don't believe it! The truth of the matter remains: Americans are very unforgiving people! This sounds like a contradiction in terms, but it's not. And the reason is that we tend to be much more forgiving of other people than we are of *ourselves!*

That is the real secret underlying the old adage. Let me take the liberty of rephrasing it: To err is human, to forgive *yourself,* divine!

Think about it. Isn't it true? Are you not a much more harsh critic of yourself than of anyone else? Isn't it true that you have frequently felt extremely guilty about actions which, if they were committed by anyone else, you'd laugh at and say they were foolish to be so torturing themselves? Of course you have.

Guilt is unquestionably one of the most serious and insidious of the eleven deadly sins of energy loss because it operates in a very cyclical fashion. In time it becomes very difficult to even remember where the chain reaction began.

But it's important, very important, to pinpoint the sources of your own needless guilt. Because not only is guilt needless; worse, it is destructive. The following are a few examples of the kind of things over which people I know and have worked with have typically felt guilty. Read this brief list, then think about the sources of your own guilt.

*Many men feel guilty about not being more financially successful—despite the fact that their families and friends frequently admire them for doing as well as they are. Nevertheless, they berate themselves that they haven't accomplished more, don't have more savings in the bank, more life insurance, more equity, you name it.

33

*Many women feel guilty about not being worldly-wise, knowledgeable, informed, and intellectually up-to-date. They feel guilty about being "stupid." Despite the fact that they are bright, that they run their daily affairs with infinite common sense and astuteness, that they are reading and thinking all the time, they somehow cavalierly toss off these things as though they didn't matter—and feel guilty and inadequate.

*Many people feel guilty because they are less physically attractive than they would like to be.

*Some people feel guilty because they suspect they are not as romantic as someone else.

*Others feel guilty because they assume they are bad mothers or fathers.

*Still others feel guilty that they didn't got to college. Or that they didn't finish college. Or that they spent too long in college and graduate school. Or that they stayed too long in the employ of the company for which they are now working. Or that they are forcing their children to live in a bad environment.

The choices, the options, we have for feeling guilty are endless—infinite! Think about it. If any of us wanted to, if any of us were not careful, would it not be possible to feel guilty because we were simultaneously a bad parent, an unsatisfactory breadwinner, a poor spouse, a lousy friend, a social bore, an intellectual blob, a physical has-been and on and on and on. Sound silly? Perhaps. But now let's get down to cases. Yours.

Don't try to inventory everything which you may feel guilty about—try to focus in on the two or three *major* sources of your own guilt feelings. Don't think about whether you should or shouldn't feel guilty about these things, just select the particular aspects of yourself which make you feel the

34

most guilty. Now on a new page in your diary under the heading: "Things Which Make Me Feel Guilty," write down the two or three major sources of your own guilt feelings.

For example, you might write: "I don't earn enough money." "I lack self-discipline." "I am sloppy in my housekeeping." "I am a poor wife." "I am not as sexually alive as I should be." "I drink too much." "I am intellectually unstimulating."

These above are just a few examples: the things which you have felt guilty about may be quite different. Choose the shoe that fits.

Again, just write a simple one-line subheading and leave a third or half page underneath it. Now, take the first thing that you wrote down, and still being very honest with yourself, put down the approximate amount of time that you have felt this way about yourself. In other words, if you wrote down, "I am not as sexually alive as I should be," think to yourself, "How long have I felt this way?" A year? Five years? Always?

After writing down the approximate amount of time you have felt this negative way about yourself, think about the forms this feeling may assume. Does the feeling cause you to be tight inside? Restless? Nervous? Jumpy? Tired?

All right. Write down under the thing you felt guilty about and the amount of time you have felt that way, the various ways that this guilt manifests itself—the way guilt is expressed in your own behavior. This may seem difficult, but you've got to write it down. By following these instructions step-by-step, you will force yourself to come to grips with wasted energy. If you try to skip over this step, you'll sweep your guilt into a corner and will never clear out the sludge from the human engine which energizes your lifestyle.

If you did follow instructions, you may have written down something like this: "Feeling this way makes me tense and upset and then I avoid doing the thing which would cause me to relax. I don't do the things I should. I postpone things. I get so bogged down in feeling guilty that I get immobilized. I can't do anything. I just sit there like a lump on a log."

That's right, you're not unique. These are exactly the ways guilt manifests itself.

Now, after you've made some notes under each of the two or three main things you feel guilty about, write down the name of the person who either directly or indirectly made you feel guilty about this particular aspect of yourself. Again, be absolutely, brutally frank with yourself. The feeling may be associated with somebody who is no longer exerting a direct influence on your life. Perhaps, for example, a dead parent or a former husband, long since divorced. Or maybe you'll come up with no outsider, no *other* person. Maybe it was *you,* you yourself, that caused you to feel guilty about this aspect of yourself. If such is the case, write down "me."

Now, we'll try to get at at least one fundamental cause for each major guilt feeling. Have you ever stumbled on this basic truth that underlies all human guilt feeling: *the feeling of guilt involves an implicit comparison.* A comparison to what? Invariably, the answer is: *to a certain standard.*

That's right, it's that simple. You wouldn't experience the feeling of guilt if you weren't comparing yourself to something, if you weren't holding your behavior up against some benchmark. Whether that standard has been conscious or unconscious before today doesn't matter. I tell you with unalterable conviction that if you think about it hard and long enough, you will realize I am right. I have conducted this exercise over a period of thirteen years with more than three thousand men and women. And typically, when I ask them to tell me what is the standard against which they are comparing or evaluating their everyday behavior, they look at me blankly. They say such things as, "What do you mean Dr. Mok? There's no standard, no comparison. I've just always felt guilty about not being brighter—about not having developed myself more intellectually."

But every major guilt has its source—its root cause. Frequently there is multiple causation. For instance, in the case of one individual who told me there was no standard against which he was comparing himself, I had the time and opportunity to probe more deeply. How long had he felt this particular way? For more than twenty years, it turned out, ever since high school. As we explored the matter mutually, he went on to say that his older brother had gone to medical school and that when his father had died, he dropped out of his second year of college and went into industrial sales. Further, honest introspection caused him to realize that both his parents had imposed upon him very high standards for intellectual achievement, that he had internalized these standards (making them his own), and that at the age of nineteen or twenty, he had begun thinking of himself as a failure—as somehow damaged—because he hadn't gone on and gotten a bachelor's certificate to put on the wall and a *Phi Beta Kappa* key to put on a watch chain.

Now, I want you to think back on your own major guilt feelings and try to pinpoint a major source. You have to go further now. What expectations did that key person—or did you yourself—have for you? Try to translate this standard into a sentence or two about what they—or you—expect. You might write down, "My father expected me to be brilliant." "I expected I would be making $30,000 by the time I was thirty." "I expected I would always have a lot of dates, a lot of men calling me up, just as I did in college." "I expected to be free of major financial worries by the time I was forty." "My wife expects me to build up her savings account as well as my own." "I always expected I'd be patient as a parent and do a lot of fun things with my children." I know it's hard to be this brutally honest with yourself, but it's necessary, I assure you.

Now comes the interesting and perhaps most self-revealing and illuminating part. Take a few notes under each major guilt feeling about the basic standard of comparison or self-expectation. Ask yourself this question: If I bared my true feelings to the three people whose opinions I most respect, would they think I was right or wrong in feeling so guilty about this particular aspect of my personality or behavior?

Stop. Don't jump to conclusions. Write down the names of those three trusted individuals. Next to each name, mentally making the assumption that you asked this person the above-stated question, would he or she say you were right or wrong. Most of you will come out wrong across the board. The reason is quite simple. The reasons we think of ourselves as failing lie *not in our inadequate behavior, but in the unrealism of our internalized self-expectations*. If you perhaps answered affirmatively next to any of the three names, I invite you to do something which might seem harder, but which might prove quite rewarding. Without revealing to that trusted individual in the next week that you are engaged in the serious process of recycling your life style, engage him or her in an informal conversation, saying that you've been thinking about yourself lately—and a couple of your so-called hangups— and mention one or two of the things that you feel guilty about. Don't even say why you've raised the subject. Just say something like this: "You've known me quite awhile, you've seen me in informal situations as I really am, what's your reaction to this particular feeling on my part?" I'll give you odds that the individual is surprised. Either he or she will find it difficult even to imagine that you have felt guilty about this aspect of yourself or, if he or she is not surprised, will probably say something like, "You're being ridiculous. Why do you berate yourself? Good heavens, I'm not as strong as you are in that respect, and I don't feel guilty."

3. *Anger*——Anger has many forms from mild irritation to wild rage. Hardly a day goes by in the life of any of us when we don't, at least for a moment, feel angry about something. But I want you to think now not about minor irritations, but serious feelings of anger.

The serious anger feelings we experience tend to be predictable, virtually chronic. In other words, a certain situation almost invariably causes us to be angry. Or some other individual with whom we have a close relationship does a particular thing which invariably makes us angry. Or, a certain frequently executed action of our own makes us feel angry with ourselves. Anger is a serious deadly sin not because it is experienced—that is very healthy and normal—but because *it feeds on itself!*

Let me show you what I mean. Let's say a man

who works very hard typically feels quite angry at his wife about the way she handles money. Now, it would be quite healthy if he confronted her on a given day with an impulsive purchase that she had made and said, "I am angry and upset that you bought this particular item. We don't really need it and can't afford it at this time. I want you to take it back."

But suppose, on the other hand, as is frequently the case, this man felt so overwhelmed with anger, so boiling mad, that he did not even trust himself to say anything to his wife. What happens? The anger of the moment recedes, but does it vanish? No, it becomes reduced to a sense of resentment. Resentment builds upon resentment. Layers of resentment fan the flames of new anger when a similar event occurs. The problem becomes compounded. Soon a serious conflict exists.

All of us have seriously angry feelings which for one reason or another we have not dealt with effectively. And the failure to deal with hostility effectively robs us of beautiful creative energy.

Back to your diary. On a separate page, write the heading *People and Situations Which Make Me Angry*. Write down, leaving a space under each, the two or three individuals who have caused you to feel most angry during the past several months. That's right, write down their actual names. Underneath each name, write what they do that causes you to feel most furious. Your list might look something like this:

1. My boss, John Callahan

It makes me furious when he asks me, time after time, to work overtime during the evening or on weekends at no extra pay. It makes me angry that he never compliments me on the good work that I do.

2. My husband

He makes me angry when he always finds fault. He's never satisfied. He's so picky.

3. My teenage son, Robert

It makes me furious that he's so inconsiderate. He never volunteers to do anything to help the family. It makes me angry that he's so lazy.

I am sure it shouldn't be hard for you to think of two or three people that make you most angry—or what they do that causes you to be upset. Have you written down the names of the people and what they've done? If not, do it now, because all of these notations in your diary will be helpful not only immediately but in coming weeks or months when you run self-checks on whether you're effectively recycling your lifestyle. It's important to have a base line of comparison on a realistic and self-objective basis from the time when you first started thinking and doing something about improving your lifestyle in a permanent way.

Now, under each anger-provoking situation, list your own typical behavioral response to this situation. Don't kid yourself, now. Put down what actually happens, what you typically do.

Your list might look something like this: "I get so exasperated, I just walk out of the room." "Sometimes I become so upset, I blow my cool and burst into tears." "Usually I holler and shout, sometimes say things I regret later." "I try to point out to the person what he's done wrong, but it doesn't do any good." "I complain in a polite way, then walk away and find myself getting much more upset later in the evening." "I feel my stomach rolling over, my insides are tied up in knots and I don't even feel like eating."

Now go back to your diary and under each main provoking person, situation and response, write down: "Which was more destructive—the provoking individual's behavior—or my response to it?" Then write your answer.

Surprised? Probably not. But it's food for thought, isn't it? That a major cause of curtailed lifestyle is not the outsider, the someone else, or even the irritating things he does, but the way you handled the situation—your response to it. Go back to each section on the anger page in your diary and spend a few moments thinking about ways you could handle your own anger more effectively, ways you might respond in the future which would be different and get you out of the box of resentment. Whether you will be able to do these more effective things right away is not as important for the moment as becoming increasingly self-aware and self-objective. Just having a few notes down in black and white will serve as healthy reminders to you when you find yourself in a similar situation next time.

4. *Self-Blame*——The most insidious part of self-blame is that fact that the process is passive. If blaming yourself typically caused you to remove a roadblock to growth, to feel more relaxed or to experience increased satisfaction, I would be all in favor of it.

But self-blame does not operate this way. What happens, in fact, could be more accurately described as a vicious cycle. For example, you overindulge at a social gathering on a Friday night. You wake up Saturday feeling rocky and you begin torturing yourself: 'Why did I do it? What was wrong with me? I know I made an ass of myself. Your self-recrimination makes you feel doubly heavy, doubly guilty. You worry. You agonize. Now, for the next two hours, perhaps all day Saturday, you'll find it impossible to climb out of this self-imposed fog.

Another example. You said something unkind to a co-worker on the spur of the moment and you realize you hurt the other person—you were probably wrong. Instead of letting it go, instead of filing it if not forgetting it and making amends in a constructive way—instead of objectively realizing that the other person probably quickly regained equilibrium, you now start berating yourself. *How could I have been so unkind? What's wrong with me? She'll never forgive me. I'm really a bitch.* And so on.

So what happens? All day long you feel loggy or nervous. You avoid the children. You ask your husband to do the chores because you are too upset. You start casting up other things that you did wrong. Other examples of inconsiderateness. Soon you find yourself getting really depressed. And so it goes.

In your notebook, put the word *Self-Blame* at the top of a new page. Skip several lines and then write down these words: "Blaming myself without taking constructive corrective action is a sin. It saps vital, creative energy resources. I hereby resolve not to play the self-flagellation game any longer. I will make amends when I can, but I will not waste Saturday's energy in self-recrimination for what I did on Friday!"

5. *Fear*——We've all heard the saying, "Man is his own worst enemy." There is a lot of truth in this saying, and one of the major reasons has to do with fear. Everyone of us is afraid of something—of old age, of losing youth and attractiveness, of economic insecurity, or rejection. The list is infinite.

It's easy to see that being afraid is normal. The fact of being afraid does not in itself constitute a stumbling block. The problem lies in how we deal with our feelings of being afraid.

Again, I invite you to look at yourself dispassionately. Think, if you will, of the two things that cause you to be most afraid. They can be things that are happening right now in your life, things that you anticipate in the near future, possibilities down the road. On a new page in your diary write the heading: *"My Fears—And How I Handle Them."* Near the top of the page under the heading, write down the thing that frightens you most. Leave half a page of blank space, then write the second most significant fear in your life right now. Go back to the first listed fear and make some notes in the following vein: how long have you had this fear; what are its main apparent causes; how much time on a daily basis would you estimate you've thought about this particular fear; what forms did the feeling assume (in other words, was it self-dialogue, nervousness, irritability, loss of sleep, poor appetite, palpitations, excessive smoking, insomnia?); what were the positive or negative consequences of these fear translations. Under your paragraph of notes, write this question: "Do I wish to go on forever responding this way?" Write down your answer. I am sure it will be negative.

I am sure that this exercise, like the others, has been self-instructive. If you've performed it honestly and systematically, you should now realize that the basis of your innermost fears is probably valid, that there is a realistic reason for you to be concerned. However, what you should also be able to see is that the way the fear translates itself into everyday behavior on your part is destructive rather than constructive.

Coming to grips with a strong fear sometimes seems hopeless. But it isn't. Not if you proceed logically and unemotionally. Unfortunately, that's exactly what most of us typically do *not* do. We dwell on our fears and we let them control our behavior. If, on the other hand, we check these self-destructive behavioral translations, we might not eliminate the sources of fear, but we could be successful in stopping them from robbing our vital creative energy resources.

In other words, I am asking you to install a mental burglar-alarm system to prevent energy loss due to fear. Go back now to your diary and write, "What things could I do differently to control these self-destructive behavioral translations?" "What things could I do to stop my fear from overwhelming me like a gigantic tidal wave?" Then write down your suggested corrective controls.

Your list might read something like this: "When I first start dwelling on this particular fear, I will check myself, realizing that otherwise I'll fall into the bottomless pit. I will deliberately force myself to seek the companionship of others when I start feeling this way. I will try to deflect my attention even if it means watching television, going out to the movies or calling someone I like on the telephone. I will temporarily suspend that awful worrying feeling and talk with those I trust tomorrow and see how they are handling their serious fears and concerns. I will remember that I am not alone, that others have lived effectively with the same fear— and so can I. If there is a particular activity in which I typically find solace, I will instantly turn to that rather than allowing the fear to immobilize me.

45

I'll listen to a record of Beethoven or the Beatles, I'll read my favorite Psalm in the Bible, I'll play gin rummy with a friend or I'll watch the late movie on television."

These things may sound silly now when you are not feeling victimized by your own fears. Believe me, however, when I say they won't seem silly at all a few nights from now when the rain is battering against the window and the wind is howling and that old familiar spectre returns to haunt you.

Self-Punishment——It's probably dawned on you by now—if it hadn't in the past—that all of these worry mechanisms, all of these negative forces, involve a self-punitive aspect. You know that you have been punishing yourself, but do you know why?

Surprisingly, few people do.

I believe that it goes back to something quite puritanical in our culture: the notion that all of our badness, all of our mistakes and wrong-doing must somehow be expiated. It has to do with ancient authoritarian aspects of family living and society.

Let me give you a down-to-earth example. When you were a child and you did something wrong— you were disobedient, you did something dishonest, you physically hurt a brother or sister, you verbally assaulted someone, you failed to do your homework assignments—what happened? Like as not, one of your parents punished you. Physically, verbally, nonverbally—for the moment it doesn't matter— the essential point is that some authority imposed a punishment upon you. Having thus served the meted-out punishment, you were free to go on your whistling way. You wrote lines on the blackboard in school. You sat in a corner. You took your whipping and didn't flinch. You took your tongue-lashing. You promised not to commit the particular sin again.

So a cycle was established: unacceptable behavior, authoritarian punishment, and then absolution from guilt. But what happened to you when you grew up, became an adult, and there was no longer a scowling authority to mete out punishments which represented the necessary middle link before you could receive absolution?

You punished yourself instead. That's right. That's what we all do. However, no matter how harsh the authoritarian figure of earlier years, your own built-in authoritarian voice is stronger, more critical, harder to please. Instead of giving yourself a five-minute tongue-lashing, you torture yourself silently in a seemingly endless dialogue that lasts for days and maybe even weeks.

The school of psychology called *transactional analysis* has shown us that in each one of us—restricting the growth of the healthy energetic adult we should be—are two other "persons": a spoiled, self-indulgent child and a mean, angry unforgiving parent. So much vitally valuable energy and time is tragically wasted in the warfare between these "two other persons" in your psyche!

Back to your diary. New page. At the top write the heading *"My Own Self-Punishment Mechanism."* On the next line write the phrase: "Other Person Number One. The Spoiled, Self-Indulgent Child in Me." Leave a half page of blank space and in the middle of the page put down, "Other Person Number Two. The Angry, Unforgiving Parent in Me." Go back to the top of the page and think about some of the childish, selfish, mean, nasty or otherwise self-indulgent things you've done lately. I know it hurts, but write them down anyway.

Your list might contain items like this: "I overate all week long and gained four pounds this past week." "I got drunk on Thursday night, couldn't even wait for the weekend." "I blew all my pin money on two new dresses, didn't have a dime left over for anything else." "Lost fifteen dollars playing gin rummy on the train." "Spent more money on the cabin—I'm the only one that even likes it."

I am sure you could list half a dozen things, but you don't have to put down that many, just enough to get the idea across to yourself. Now for the reprisals. Beginning at the middle of the page under the heading, "Other Person Number Two. The Angry, Unforgiving Parent in Me," list the things you told yourself, did, tried to do, or have been thinking about as means of punishment for the sins listed on the top of the page.

Your list might read something like this: "I cheated on my expense account to get back the money I lost playing gin rummy." "I gave one of the dresses I bought to my daughter or friend." "I got so mad at myself for having put on four extra pounds that I drank too much and put on another two pounds." "I swore I'd sell the cabin this year." "I told my spouse I was turning over a new leaf."

Now, if there is any space left at the bottom of this diary page, write the question, "How constructive were these efforts at self-correction?" If you're honest, you will probably have written something like this: "Zilch—I was only kidding myself, damn it!"

Now turn the page. At the top write this heading: "Things I Can Do to Break Out of the Bad Child/Punitive Parent Syndrome."

Think about it a few minutes. Take your time; go slowly. Do you see the point? I am sure you do. Instead of getting into the game in the first place, the healthy adult in you has said, "Maybe I don't even have to play this game at all."

Well and good. But what would getting out of the game, breaking out of the cycle, involve? It would involve imposing behavioral controls on the spoiled, self-indulgent child in yourself. Preventing the impulsive acting-out events which, in turn, trigger the self-punitive reactions.

Of course, this is easier to say than to do. I want you to do more than pay lip service to committing yourself to the concept of increased behavioral controls. In order to make the leap from nonproductive lip-service concept to meaningful corrective action, you ought to mentally review for several moments your own personal associations to the word *control*.

I've tried this out recently on twenty individuals, all friends, both male and female. Eighteen out of twenty came up with initially negative reactions. I asked them to give me the first three words they thought of when I mentioned the word *control*. Their responses included: lack of freedom, restriction, confinement, punishment, distrust, straightjacket, shackles, handcuffs, authoritarian, corporate employer and government.

If some of your own personal associations to the word *control* are akin to those I've listed, I can predict that if you thought about the matter no further, you'd *never* break out of the cycle of destructive self-punishment.

That's because the kind of control I am speaking about is fundamentally and absolutely positive. But you have to understand why this particular meaning is positive—and really believe it—if you are going to make the healthy adult within you victorious.

Sure, everyone of us feels at times like a little boy or girl. We want to indulge ourselves. Depending on our pleasure, our past conditioning, and our pocketbook we might feel like plunging into a double banana-split, a double and very dry vodka martini, into Gimbels East for a shopping spree, into a second helping of delicious casserole. Such desires are absolutely normal. But must the feeling dictate our actions?

Of course not. You feel like punching the boss in the mouth and knocking out his teeth—indeed, that can also be a very normal feeling—but you don't translate it into tooth-knocking-out action for obvious reasons. You might also feel like getting blind, staggering drunk and then driving home and going to bed. But the healthy adult in you reminds you that you don't like to make that much of an ass out of yourself, you wouldn't enjoy the hangover, and like as not you'd probably wrap your car around the telephone pole, which would hardly prove satisfying. So you don't do it.

Unfortunately, millions of Americans have been sold a gigantic bill of goods—countless lies and deceptions—about this question of control. God knows how many goody manufacturers there are who constantly plead with us through their multimillion-dollar advertising budgets: "indulge, indulge, indulge."

Do it now, think later. Spoil yourself rotten to the core. Go to the health farm. Stop at the boutique. Pamper yourself. Lounge in the sauna. Drink soft whiskey. Eat the whole thing. You can belch your way to prosperity today, there is always an antidote tomorrow.

So it goes. America's gigantic advertising industry has co-opted transactional analysis and fans the flames of the game. Scores of consumer package goods manufacturers consult with motivational psychologists to think up tricky new ways to get you to indulge the spoiled brat in you. And an equal number of consumer package goods manufacturers consult other teams of motivational psychologists to sell you drugs, relief tablets, diet foods, home exercise gyms, garage saunas, and girdles to aid the angry punitive parent in you.

Who needs it? You don't—not any longer!

7. *Anxiety*——When I was a young lieutenant in the Air Force, after every payday there were many floating crap games going on in the barracks on my base. There was one sergeant of my acquaintance who lost every cent of his pay like clockwork on the first night of the month in these games. I knew he was a loser, he knew he was a loser, but what I couldn't figure out was *why*?

Who would deliberately choose to go broke every month? Who would want to experience this much deprivation and pain? It didn't make sense. Since the sergeant was a friend of mine, I asked him point-blank one day. I'll never forget his answer: "Lieutenant, if I ever found myself on any average day of the month with money in my pocket, I wouldn't think I was still in the service." Put that in your briar and smoke it.

The thing I've realized ever since is how commonly so many of us fundamentally accept anxiety as an inevitable way of life. I imagine my poor sergeant friend was cryptically suggesting that if he did find himself with money in his pocket, he'd think for an instant he was back in civilian life and the shock of discovering he wasn't would be just too overwhelming to deal with. By insuring that he was constantly broke, no matter the anxiety involved, at least he reminded himself where he was, so to speak.

Day after day I encounter quivering executives, uptight secretaries, worried teenagers, nervous mothers, anxious college students. Ask any one of them what the trouble is. Like as not, they'll blink, and say, "Trouble? Just being an executive makes me nervous." Or, "I am a mother—that's all—naturally I'm nervous." Or, "If I didn't have hang-ups, I wouldn't be a teenager."

See what I mean? *We fundamentally accept the inevitability of our own anxieties.* Once having done so, anxiety feeds on itself. Anxiety leads to anxiety and becomes a self-fulfilling prophecy. How much anxiety is necessary? How much of it do you really want in your daily life? How much is anxiety robbing you? How much vital creative energy is being deflected in your life—on a daily basis—in mindless, unnecessary, wheel-spinning anxiety? Probably a good deal more than you've realized.

Back to your diary. New page. Put the subtitle at the top, "My Anxieties and How I Handle Them." Leaving space, write down the three things that you are most anxious about right now. Your list might contain such notations as: "I am most anxious about getting a promotion—by boss has said nothing about it to me." "I am anxious about the possibility of having to take out another bank loan." "I am anxious about passing this term." "I am anxious about the summer—I don't know whether we'll be able to have a vacation." "I am most anxious about what top management really thinks of me—and my potential."

I only want you to list three major sources of anxiety. Now, under each, write down the behavioral forms into which the anxiety is typically translated.

The student, for example, if he were being candid and objective with himself—as I hope you will be—might write: "I lose a lot of sleep worrying about whether I'll pass. Having lost sleep, I've missed a few classes. I've asked a couple of friends to let me borrow their notes. I've thought to myself what I would tell my parents if I were put on probation."

The young manager concerned about whether he will be promoted might have in his diary something like this: "I guess I've acted up-tight with the people in the office. I've acted more moody lately with my secretary. I've stayed late at the office, but I haven't gotten much done. I have probably taken it out in drinking a little more heavily lately. I haven't been much fun with the kids. I am getting snappy with my wife over little unimportant things. I have tried to find out on the grapevine if other people at my level have been promoted, but it's like a no-man's land. This causes me to worry even more."

In order to recycle your lifestyle, you must learn not to feel anxious. Examine very seriously and objectively what the behavioral consequences of your anxieties really are. You'll see that they add up to nothing more nor less than a considerable waste of valuable time and vital energy. Compounding the felony, as it were, they create additional problems, the knowledge of which causes you to experience additional guilt and worry, which, in turn, leads to self-blame, self-punishment, and more anxiety.

On the same page in the diary, try to approximate the relative amount of time, on a daily basis, you've invested in nonconstructive response to your anxieties. List the net consequences of these responses.

Then, on a fresh page, challenge yourself as follows: "Ways I might handle or respond to my anxieties more effectively."

Your list might run something like this: "Instead of burying my anxiety inwardly, or acting out in moody ways with other people, I will seek more direct confrontation and feedback with key persons. I will not make others the victims of my moods. Drinking is a worthless and self-destructive antidote to anxiety—I will remember that and control my behavior accordingly. Instead of thinking in terms of tackling the whole problem in one day, I will address myself to specific small constructive steps I can take toward getting out of the bind."

Later I will ask you to track or monitor your behavioral pattern, since only by so doing will you be able to see whether you are really recycling your lifestyle or falling back into the same conditioned, destructive and negative mechanisms.

8. *Assumed Failure*——Most people fail because they don't try—or they only try half-heartedly. But why don't we try—and why is it that even if a particular goal is meaningful to us, we approach it with only a half-hearted effort? The answer is simple but very far-reaching: we fail before we fail.

In other words, before we try, we assume we will fail. Assuming we will fail to achieve the particular goal, we either eliminate any effort, which allows us the childlike rationalization, "Well, I could have done that if I had wanted to, but I didn't really want to," or we deceive ourselves into thinking that we're really trying when in fact we are only approaching the task or the goal on three of our proverbial eight cylinders. This also serves the defensive function of hedging our bets and allowing ourselves to rationalize that the task or goal wasn't really that important or that it was really out of reach, over our heads. Or, that it wasn't our fault that we didn't succeed, because after all we did try, didn't we? How many foremen I have known in manufacturing plants who had the knowledge and

54

skill and intelligence to become managers of technical departments but who never made it. How many times they have told me, "But I couldn't do it, Dr. Mok. The company never lets you do that." Or, "I didn't have enough education." Or, "Sure I would have liked to have become a department head or manager but they just favor young people." Or, "Let's face it, I'm not an engineer so why should I have kidded myself?"

In many of these companies, younger people were not being favored. Great efforts were being made to encourage foremen to aspire to higher positions. In many instances other foremen with no more formal education than the individuals I was interviewing had already been promoted into managerial positions and beyond. The theme was always the same: *They failed before they failed.*

The assumption of failure is truly a deadly sin because it represents nothing more nor less than a cop-out on our God-given talents, our individuality and our most valued psychic energy resource.

Go back to your diary now and list just one tough, challenging and very meaningful goal that you would like to achieve during the next year. Something you've worried a lot about being able to do. Choose something quite specific and make it a hard one, something that would be out of the ordinary and yet within realistic reach, something largely dependent upon your own efforts—a goal, the completion of which would really delight and exhilarate you. After you've listed this specific goal, make a list under this subheading: "Reasons I May Not Make It." You might list things like: "I don't think I'll get the additional resources; there really isn't enough time; my company hasn't made it clear whether it's really one hundred per cent committed to this particular goal; no one else at my level has ever done it; I'm handling so many other things I just may not be able to push hard enough; my everyday essential activities will bog me down or hold me back." And so on. Now skip several spaces and a third of the way down the page make notes under this heading: "My Major Self-Attitudinal Stumbling Block."

Here you might make such notes as: "My own underlying lack of confidence." "Fear that I may not be bright enough to handle it on my own." "My own lack of drive," "My tendency to procrastinate." "A tendency to get preoccupied with details which may retard my progress." "My own difficulty in selling other people on my ideas."

I think you are beginning to see the point. The reasons we usually give for failure tend to be lumped under the first category—the outside factors—external circumstances.

But the true reasons for failure are usually not those given first, but those held back. The fears, the anxieties, the personal internal stumbling blocks. Now draw a circle around the personal stumbling block or self-attitudinal barrier which you honestly believe could be most destructive of your chances for success.

Now I tell you this—and heed it—if you spend but twenty minutes per day working on your own self-attitudinal barrier, reducing that down to size and getting through it or above it, you will succeed!

You may not believe it now. That's because the old self-attitudinal barrier is still operating. It isn't going to disappear merely because I tell you so. But if you're really serious about recycling your lifestyle, you'll have no difficulty in capturing vital energy and time that was previously wasted in preoccupying yourself with your mistakes, and blaming yourself, and punishing yourself and so on. The opportunity is staring you in the face.

Stop rationalizing. Go back to your diary page and write down some self-imposed suggestions for handling the self-attitudinal barrier you've just circled.

Believe in those things that you write down. Commit yourself to them. Do them. Check yourself. Remind yourself. Come back to this page tomorrow, next week, next month. Sure it takes rigorous self-disciplined effort—but that's what recycling your lifestyle is all about.

9. *Need to Possess*——What do I mean by the need to possess? And why should this need represent one of the eleven deadly sins of energy loss? Do you think you are possessive? Perhaps not.

The truth is, we all are. We like other people to be beholden to us. It makes us feel important to do favors for others. We don't start out by seeking to live their lives, to control their destinies, but very often—probably much more so than you realize—the things we do under the banner of good intentions, sincerity, and interest in others really represent our own insecure quests toward feeling important. Let me give you a few common examples. They may not be things which you've actually done, but don't be misled if any of my examples are exaggerated—it's the underlying mechanism I want you to understand and look at.

Every night a mother reviews the homework of her thirteen-year-old son. She corrects it word by word, example by example. What he does not know she tells him. If you ask her why she is doing this, her answer will be, "I'm just trying to help him. I want him so much to succeed." If you told this mother, "you are being inordinately possessive, you are swallowing up your child, you are making it difficult for him to learn and become self-reliant," what would she say? She'd say, "You don't want me to let him fall on his face, do you? Shouldn't a parent show an interest in her child's learning?"

Another example. A young couple moves into your apartment building and you become friendly with them. They don't have much furniture and they welcome your ideas about decorating their apartment. Because you want to help, you give them some slipcovers you were planning to throw away. You remember a couple of pieces of discarded furniture—a bookcase and an end table. They appear very grateful. You speak to the young wife daily on the telephone. How is she progressing? Is there anything further you can do to help? You engage her in long discussions about her progress, her plans, her intentions, whether she intends to buy or make draperies, whether you could help her. While you are downtown, you happen to see a large oil painting which would go just beautifully over the couch which is now sporting the slipcovers you gave the young couple.

Again, because you want to be helpful and you are very sincere in this positive and good intention, you purchase the painting for the young couple and give it to them with a great deal of enthusiasm. You offer to help hang it over their couch. They seem nonplussed, bewildered. Less enthusiastic and grateful than you would expect. You become angry with them. What's the matter, are they ingrates? That painting cost quite a bit of money, don't they realize that? Days pass. When you stop down at their apartment you notice the painting has not been hung. You comment on its absence. Where is it, you wonder. The wife seems befuddled. "Oh, George put it to one side—somewhere—I forget."

Now suppose in one single, shattering moment of candor the young wife said to you something like this: "You and your husband are driving us crazy! What's the matter—do you want to run our lives? Sleep in our beds, chew our food for us? You are swallowing us up. You're so possessive. We appreciate your help, or at least we did at first, but now you're driving us to distraction. Why don't you just live your lives and let us live ours. Don't call us, we'll call you!" You'd be floored. How unjust. How inconsiderate. How selfish and immature.

Alas, it's true. We are all possessive—all acting out our need to be important at the expense of other people, frequently those we love best. We fail to see the often fragile line between helping and swallowing—between responding to a need and taking over.

Why do we do this? Where does the need to possess come from?

Basically it comes from childhood and from insecurity. It comes from the need to possess the love of others. An obvious way to earn and possess love, we learn as children, is to do good things.

Therefore as we grow older and become adults we seek to possess land, equity, things, friends, strangers. Anything attractive around us, inanimate or animate, can become a target, a prize for us to possess. If we possess this thing or this person's love or respect, it will prove to us that we are good— that we are truly lovable. Then we will be able to be secure. At last!

Ironic as it may seem, many, if not most, exaggerated displays of goodness are really reflections of the giver's insecurity—of his need to swarm over people, to swallow them up, to have them be beholden to him, to have them become a living, walking, talking testimony to his benevolence.

I'm not suggesting that you become a taker instead of a giver. I'm not suggesting that you curb normal generosity. I am asking you, on the other hand, to be realistic and objective with yourself about this tendency to overdo—to overcontrol, through good intent, the lives of others.

If you have not unwittingly fallen into this trap, so much the better; you will not have to use your diary at this time. But some of us—the oversolicitous mother, now widowed, who calls her thirty-year-old son three times a day *simply because she is worried about his health and well-being*; the executive who has groups of young managers come out to his house every weekend for barbecues and good fellowship *simply because he wants to assure them that management really cares about their progress*; the secretary who must go out with three different young men each weekend, whether she likes them or not, *simply because it's important to be seen at parties*—are wasting valuable creative energy resources in the need to possess. And worse, they may not even know it!

If the shoe fits—and if you think maybe it does a little bit—I suggest that you make an entry in your diary titled, "My Need to Be Possessive." Write down with whom you have been possessive during the past two or three months. It may be your husband or wife, your children or your closest friends. Write down the forms, the behavioral translations this possessiveness has already assumed.

Your list might contain items like these: "calling them on the telephone too frequently; making one or two unexpected visits per day; inviting them to our house every weekend like clockwork; going out as a double date foursome every time we go someplace." Then skip several spaces and jot down a few introspective notes under: "Reasons I Tend to Behave This Way." You don't have to do a long or deep self-analysis to come up with one or two major causative factors. Skip several spaces and then write down "Negative Consequences of My Possessiveness."

You'll soon discover that not only are you likely to be irritating the persons you love, but also that you are deflecting valuable creative energies which more properly should be channeled into self-development activities. If you were not going to lean on this other person or persons in quite so possessive a fashion, what things might you do with the two or three hours saved each week to make yourself feel fulfilled? Write these down. They'll become important benchmarks in your quest toward recycling your own lifestyle.

10. *Overreactions*——Overreactions are emotional responses which are appropriate in kind but excessive in degree.

For example, if you told your child to pick up and put away his dirty clothes, and half an hour later they were still lying on the floor, it would be appropriate for you to be irritated and to vent this emotion. Tell the youngster in a firm voice to pick up the things this minute and see to it that he does. Fine.

But suppose in that situation you absolutely blew your stack and screamed and cursed at your youngster for ten full minutes. Suppose you said you were absolutely appalled by his unconscionable behavior, that he was an absolutely filthy little slob, that he was obviously trying to unglue your mind completely and send you screaming and crying to the booby-hatch, that you will not tolerate this behavior for an instant longer, that he is exactly like his slob of a father, and that you wish he would walk out in the street and get run over by a truck so that you'd never have any of his dirty laundry to face ever again. Well, I doubt that many of us would react quite that way. But if we did, that would certainly be an overreaction.

Most of us overreact several times every day. Somebody does a relatively minor thing to irritate you and you lambaste them as though they had tried to commit murder. Or somebody shows up fifteen minutes late for a lunch date and you get so busy psychoanalyzing them you forget to eat lunch. Or your youngster gets a low grade on a test and you have a half-hour, heart-to-heart discussion with him in which you talk about the statistics of educational drop-outs, impress upon him that you don't want him to become a gasoline station attendant, that this behavior is the first obvious signal of an underlying antiestablishment posture and that you don't want him to become a bearded hippy and draft evader.

Sure, it's easy to see how overreactive we all are. But it seems so silly, so absurd to behave in these ways. Why then do we do it? Usually the reasons are quite complex, buried beneath our consciousness. We don't always overreact. Each of us is inclined, predictably, to overreact more to some situations than to others. To some people more than to others. Why?

It has to do with our underlying values. Our bedrock assumptions about morality—good and evil. If you examine your own overreaction pattern scientifically, you'll see what I mean.

Take the woman who chronically overreacts when

her children are careless and sloppy. What really bothers her are not the actions themselves but what they symbolize. Their behavior symbolizes to her—at an unconscious level—a repudiation of *her* basic values, a repudiation of authority and order. At a gut level she is disturbed by many things happening in our society—and perhaps very validly and understandably so. She absolutely believes in the value of individual responsibility and obedience. She sees irresponsibility and disobedience rampant in her society. At a gut level she feels the world is coming apart. Anarchy is not a real possibility, it is already here! If this is her attitude, in terms of her underlying values, she will likely see the children's sloppiness as a fundamental test not only of herself, but of those values she most cherishes. And understandably she overreacts. But what happens once she does?

Her children are likely not to be better for her overreaction. They are likely to be upset, and indeed she may have set up a subsequent tug-of-war. But worse, what happens to her in the wake of her own overreaction? She feels she was wrong to have lost her temper and screamed, to have fallen apart momentarily and blown her cool. She slides into the quiet quagmire of guilt and begins to flagellate herself and assume that there is something basically wrong with her, that she is not a good mother. Now she tortures herself at night, guiltily brooding about her inadequacy, her failure. And valuable vital creative energy resources are deflected in the process.

Once again it's time to take out your diary. Title a new page, "My Overreactions."

Think for a few moments toward whom you have

overreacted just in the past few weeks. List only two key persons. What things have they done which have caused you to overreact? List these behaviors. Be very specific.

Skip several lines, then write down the ways in which you have overreacted. How did you translate this overreaction into behavior? Did you become moody, did you cry, did you holler, shout and scream? Did you argue? List exactly what you did in the wake of this disturbing situation. Do the same in respect to the other key person toward whom you've overreacted. List the situations and the behavioral translations of your overreaction.

Now look over the notes you have written and see if you can discover any common themes. In other words, is there a similarity in the type of situation that typically sets you off? Have your overreactions taken a certain predictable form—of shrillness, let's say, of quasi-hysteria?

If so, and such is usually the case, ask yourself the difficult question—*why?* What underlying gut values were being threatened in these situations?

They may not be readily apparent to you first crack out of the box, but think about it. Take your time. Even if you're able to identify only one underlying gut value which the irritating behaviors triggered in yourself, you've come a long way—farther than many people I have helped in clinical and counseling sessions. We are all defensive creatures and we don't like to admit our overreactions, much less to explore their possible underlying causes.

Let's assume you have been able to identify one or two underlying basic values that were thus threatened. I am not going to ask you to relinquish this value. Far from it. I want you to realize that feeling this way is one hundred per cent normal and acceptable. The problem lies not in the feeling, but in the way you translated the feeling into behavior.

Ask yourself, "When I feel so strongly and so upset—when this value is threatened in the future—how can I react differently? What things could I do to avoid such an overreaction?"

Be specific. Don't try to put a lid altogether on your feelings. See how you can control them, express them, but at less amplified volume. Not only will the situation be corrected faster with less resentment on the part of the other person, but you'll be surprised and pleased how much better you feel—and how much less guilt you will have to expiate!

. *Obsessions*——Usually when we see the word "obsession" in print, we conjure up some awful, mysterious image. An obsession is nothing that you or I would be involved in. Right?

Wrong. We all tend to be obsessed about certain things, we merely choose not to recognize the patterns as representing obsessions—because the word itself is a traditional "no no."

For example, we may be obsessed with the quest for privacy. We choose to omit the psychological label and merely say to ourselves we want to be left alone and why does every mother-loving Tom, Dick and Harry want to invade our privacy? Why don't our children knock on our door before they enter? Doesn't the world know we're thinking, hatching an idea? Brother, if that's where you are, you may be obsessed with privacy.

Let's suppose you're frugal. You keep a little notebook on every cent you spend every day. If your wife said, "Jack, why are you so obsessed with money?" you'd think she was being very unfair, right? Wrong. Chances are, Jack, you *are* obsessed with money. You just choose to believe otherwise. Which is natural. Typically an obsession represents a chronic and overdetermined pattern of behavior—a series of actions which overserve a positive and strongly held value. In other words, the energies expended in serving this particular value are either unworthy of the results obtained or, as is more frequently the case, set up a whole chain reaction of additional problems, not only in our relationships with others around us, but, in the last analysis, also for ourselves.

Think for a moment of any particular action pattern of yours which others have suggested to you may be extreme. Again, try to be subjective enough to admit certain possibilities without defensive self-justification.

Are you obsessed with your own appearance? Are you the type that feels uncomfortable if you don't change clothes at least twice a day? Does it really bother you when you see a woman with a crooked hem or a loose hairpin?

Are you obsessed with gadgets? Or with saving things? Or with your car and the way it looks?

Maybe you're not obsessed with anything—there are many people walking around who aren't. But if you are, then I'd like you to make some notes on a new diary page and list the one or two things which might be your own obsessive behavioral patterns. Think back over the past several months. How much time, on an estimate daily basis, have you spent thinking about, worrying about or acting on this particular obsession? Write down the behavioral translations—in other words, the specific things you do that reflect this underlying obsession.

You'll probably realize not that the activity was wrong, but simply that it was overdone—that the consequences or results of these behaviors were not justified on the basis of the process of concern, energy, time and activity expended to achieve them.

Ironically, many obsessions are basically strengths —or can function that way—so I am not going to ask you to erase or eliminate this particular pattern of behavior unless doing so seems warranted to you.

We've often heard the phrase, "It is necessary to build on strengths." Unfortunately, that can be very misleading. If a person builds on strength long enough and hard enough, it can become an obsession. Therefore, the road to increased effectiveness and satisfaction might not involve building on the strength or building up the strength, but rather building it down—reducing the amount of time and effort expended in the pattern. Remember, what I said in the first chapter—any virtue carried to the extreme can become a crime. Putting it another way, any positive behavioral pattern in which you're excessively involved may be doing you some self-damage. At the least, it can be robbing valuable energy which could be redirected in becoming strong in other areas that vitally need it—energy which could be otherwise used to open new vistas and fun for you.

Therefore, if you've identified yourself as having a particular obsession, I would advise you simply to list on the appropriate diary page some specific actions which you could take that would keep the pattern in better balance.

If you followed my guidance so far, congratulations! If more individuals were to embark on recycling their lifestyle with the seriousness of purpose and the objective self-scrutiny which you've already taken, a lot of psychiatric noses would be out of joint—and the world would have a much greater share of contented, relaxed and self-aware people.

3. ROADMAPS TO THE NOW AND THE NEW

How to Chart Your Present Lifestyle

Before You Decide Your New Course, You Must Determine Where You've Been

Too many times we hear things like this:

"I've decided to make myself over."

"From now on you'll see a whole new me!"

"Starting tomorrow I'm going to be an entirely different person!"

"I'm so disgusted with myself—the old me—I'm going to switch lifestyles. Just you wait and see!"

We wait. But what do we see?

We see a short spurt of frantic, forced change. Then, snap, back into the old pattern. The sheepish smile. The muttered rationalizations: outside circumstances weren't really favorable; maybe he'll try again in a few months; he *really* wanted to change, but *others* wouldn't let him; it wasn't *his* fault—could *he* help it if his efforts at change threatened those around him?

The truth of the matter remains obscured.

Our discouraged friend probably:

(1) Had not deeply thought through what lifestyle is;

(2) Did not develop a clear "map" of himself— didn't assess systematically those aspects of his past lifestyle which really satisfied him and those which dissatisfied him;

(3) Wasn't aware of how others really saw him;

(4) Was seeking to imitate someone else's lifestyle!

(5) Wanted instant success, recognition and positive feedback;

(6) Thought naively in terms of *total* change instead of a series of systematic, partial, realizable changes;

(7) Quickly became frustrated and discouraged when the events following in the wake of his decision to change didn't allow immediate achievement of his grandiose goals;

(8) Couldn't face up to the fact that he himself *wasn't truly committed* to his new lifestyle and *lacked a realistic action plan for putting it into practice*; and therefore

(9) Had to make others—the nonsympathetic *they*—the scapegoats for blame so that he could keep intact a positive, albeit probably immature and defensive, image of himself!

I have advised those seeking my professional counsel to "make haste slowly" before launching into a program of long-term self-development and change.

I caution you now to avoid the "overnight-new-me" pitfall.

Would a pilot in a strange land with a limited fuel supply merely take off and randomly fly through the sky *hoping* to arrive at the desired location? Of course not!

Yet that's precisely how many adults proceed to alter their lifestyle! Think of yourself as a pilot. Think of your behavior as your airplane engine. Think of your energy resources as the octane that activates your behavioral engine.

Before you fly off into the wild blue of new experience and activity, you'll need, just as the pilot does, to map a meaningful and well-thought-through flight plan. It's not enough to know your destination—the new lifestyle you hope to achieve. In order to get there, you'll need to map out where you are now. Once having clearly identified where you are in relation to where you've been and where you'd like to go, you'll be able to chart a realistic course.

Charting Your Present Lifestyle

Step 1. What Do Others Like About You? What Do You Like About Yourself?

Up until now you've diagnosed some of the major ways in which you've wasted valuable energy in the past. Now I'm going to ask you to flip the coin and be equally objective about some of your plus, positive behaviors. I'd like you to list these in your diary on a new page entitled, "Positive Feedback—Thing I Like About Myself."

Because we're self-critical creatures, we frequently tend to exaggerate our shortcomings and minimize our assets. *Must* you thus shortchange yourself? I don't think so.

In this era of inflation you wouldn't permit someone to shortchange you at the grocery store, would you? Of course not! You'd insist on an accurate tabulation of the items you purchased.

Well, then, I'm going to insist that you be just as accurate in tabulating positive aspects of your present lifestyle. When you think about it, you have "purchased" those behaviors, too—at the considerable expense of time, effort, trial and error, considerable experience, much feeling and thinking, and much reshaping of your behavior!

71

All right, think about yourself—*your best self!* What things have others complimented you on?

List these things. No matter what they are, no matter how seemingly insignificant. Take nothing for granted. Don't editorialize. Don't minimize. Don't hold your pencil point in the air, saying to yourself, "I shouldn't bother to list *that*, everybody does *that*. It isn't worth taking credit for." Of course it is. Not everybody *does* do *that*—and even if they did, it still would not detract from the expression of this positive behavior on your part.

Write down anything positive that comes to mind.

Have you been complimented for being attractive? For being fun to be with? For being a good friend? For a good sense of humor? For a nice speaking voice? For being a good cook? For your hobbies? The way you keep your house? For taking time out to listen to others? For being decisive? For being strong in times of crisis? For the handmade cards you send on holidays? For remembering things others have told you? For doing considerate things? For having good ideas? For the way you play golf? For being bouncy, enthusiastic? For caring about your children? For the way you make clothes? For being well informed? For telling the truth? For keeping your cool? For helping to resolve conflicts between others? For your ability to see and articulate the positions and feelings of others?

Stop! If you answered any of these questions affirmatively, write these good points down!

This is important. You may soon discover that simply by *extending* certain behavior, by doing certain things you already enjoy and do well in somewhat different contexts, you may be breaking through into a truly satisfying and exciting lifestyle!

How many things did you list?

If you enumerated fewer than ten things, stop and think again. You're probably shortchanging yourself, denying or minimizing, taking for granted as insignificant, some of your key assets. Dip into the well of your past behavior. List five or six more things.

Now look at your list with a different question in mind. *What things do I like about myself* which are not on the list? All of us do certain things, good things which have gone unnoticed, unmentioned by others— perhaps *unrevealed* to others or *insufficiently revealed*—which nevertheless are most significant. Much more than we've previously taken into account. Turn to a new diary page and list these things about yourself.

Perhaps after you've enumerated three or four such assets, your well will run dry. You'll think back about something you've already listed—something you've been complimented on—and you'll say to yourself, "I really like this aspect of me too!"

Fine. List these behaviors again and don't hesitate to describe them in slightly different words—spelling out, as accurately as you can, these self-perceived strengths.

Step 2. Refining Your Inventory of Assets

Human beings are not walking laundry lists of random positive attributes or behaviors. There are *themes* that orchestrate our daily lifestyles, that provide stability and continuity to our actions. Let's see if we can ascertain the good themes, the unifying threads, in your past positive behaviors.

I'll ask you to make two separate lists as you review and evaluate your list of strengths.

List number one we'll call *Behavioral Category*.

List number two we'll call *Essential Value*.

The following are the categories we'll use to initially refine our behavioral inventory:

I. *Behavioral Categories*

1. *Social-interpersonal*

    examples: being a good friend

    good listener

    sympathetic

    considerate of others

    fun to be with, etc.

2. *Nurturing*

    examples: doing things for others

    working for charities, good causes

    involvement in community activities

    helping others without being asked

    taking in exchange student

    teaching new skills to club members, etc.

3. *Artistic*

    examples: making unusual handicraft items

    decorating in unusual ways

    making attractive clothes

    growing pretty garden flowers

    painting

    refurbishing furniture

    making unusual cards, etc.

4. *Athletics*

    examples: playing golf, tennis, bowling

    taking long walks

    enjoying calisthenics

taking pride in being physically
fit, etc.

5. *Analytical*

    examples: enjoying problem-solving

                prefer challenging games—
bridge, chess, etc.

                enjoying complex, problem-
centered nonfiction books on
issues

                interested in helping others
identify, solve problems, etc.

6. *Achieving*

    examples: competitive hard work

                initiating new projects

                hobbies aimed at specific results

                enjoying those activities which
have tangible outcomes

                giving your all to your job, etc.

7. *Decisive*

    examples: enjoying fast-paced, competitive
situations

                cool under stress

                enjoying risk-oriented challenges

                don't become upset when forced
to take positions in complex
problem situations, despite
time, other pressures, etc.

8. *Contemplative*

    examples: enjoy being alone

                enjoying reading

                enjoying doing things at own
pace

                thoughtful

                enjoying abstract problem-solv-
ing

> integrate various kinds of ex-
> perience, data
>
> see value in doing things for
> own sake
>
> not up-tight about short-term
> results, etc.

9. *Other*

If several of your main positive feedback factors clearly aren't covered by the "umbrellas"
I've suggested, try to classify them by the
common thread or theme you feel unifies
them.

If you have categorized your list—and if your
inventory of assets was reasonably compre-
hensive—you probably discovered that your
positive behaviors are not as narrowly con-
fined as you might have thought. This is one
basic reason I asked you to perform this exercise.

Most of us are more broad-gauged than we
imagine. Certainly all of us have potential
strengths, potential for growth in behavioral
areas which heretofore represented a relative
no-man's land.

II. *Essential Value*

I ask you now to re-examine your asset inventory
and behavioral classifications.

Major areas of interest and strength represent reflections of underlying values. I won't try to suggest all
possible values which might lend shape and continuity
to your past pattern of living. But here is a list of
several major values which may reflect the things you
do most or the things you do best:

1. *Pragmatism*

The individual who has a basic underlying commitment to making things happen, to achieving and seeing tangible results, is typically expressing in a variety of behaviors the underlying essential value or commitment to pragmatism.

2. *Philosophical*

The individual who has a need to probe the reasons behind or underneath what he sees, hears, reads, observes, thinks—to question meanings, interpret life, relate what happens to what makes it happen, to integrate a vast variety of complex experience—is typically expressing his essential commitment to the value of being philosophical.

3. *Service*

The individual who seeks to extend himself or multiply what he knows or can contribute through helping others, teaching others, assisting people, helping his community or neighborhood is typically expressing his underlying commitment to the value of service.

4. *Autonomy*

The individual who expends considerable time and energy to excel independently—whether in individual sports (such as golf) or in hobbies or in his work—is typically expressing his underlying commitment to the value of being a strong autonomous individual—to the belief that his own independent growth must not be compromised.

5. *Creativity*

The individual who enjoys doing new things, developing novel or unusual ideas, problem solutions, expressing himself in artistic ways—in dress, manner, work, gardening, etc.—is typically expressing his underlying commitment to the value of creativity.

6. *Rationality*

The individual who enjoys a planned and well organized approach to life and work, who looks and looks again before he leaps, who prefers games of reason and logic to games involving a high degree of risk or intuition, who enjoys and excels at activities involving deliberation and analysis is typically expressing his commitment to the underlying value of rationality.

7. *Social*

The individual who enjoys entertaining, informal conversation, keeping abreast of what his friends, family members and business associates are doing, feeling and thinking; who enjoys sharing his own experiences with them; who believes in taking time out to relax with others, to listen to their stories, to get to know them better is typically expressing his commitment to an underlying social value.

I would like you to code or classify your inventory of assets according to the above underlying values. Once you've done this, I would like you to draw a circle around the two essential values in your own behavior pattern which you believe are strongest.

Your diary page might now look like this:

Activity	Behavior Category	Essential Value
making up new recipes	artistic, nurturing	creativity, service
good card player	social-interpersonal, analytical	social
gardening	artistic	creativity
making attractive greeting cards for family, friends	artistic	creativity
good sense of humor	social-interpersonal	social
interesting, novel ideas	artistic	creativity
helping to set up a church fair	social-interpersonal	social, service
well informed	contemplative	philosophical
good host or hostess	social-interpersonal	social
comfortable home	artistic	creativity
fun to be with	social-interpersonal	social
flexible	social-interpersonal	social
good conversationalist	social-interpersonal	social
good listener	social-interpersonal	social
considered a close friend by many people	social-interpersonal	social
good catalyst—often smooth out differences between people	social-interpersonal	social
good storyteller	artistic	creativity

Make two circles in the Essential Value column around social and creativity.

Step 3. Analysis

I have already noted that people do not act as they do by chance. Rather, we act by choice. However, a great deal of the time we're unconscious of the choices we're making. We just seem to do a thing—we're not even aware that we're making a choice.

Take the person whose assets inventory I just presented. When he or she performed gardening, did he say to himself, "I choose to do this right now. Of all the optional activities I could engage in, I am making an immediate and deliberate choice to garden!" Probably not. More likely the person just wanders out to the backyard and begins puttering around with the flowers!

Fine. But his relaxed spontaneous behavior represented a choice nevertheless. How many of us have never grown a flower in our lives? If we make hundreds of nonconscious choices every day—and all of us do—what things determine our choices?

A major such determinant is our needs. Take the individual whose assets we just examined. At the behavioral level he or she needed frequent satisfying social contact. Why? Why does one individual seemingly need a lot of friends, another very few?

The basic explanation lies not outside ourselves but rather lies in an internal need.

Let's say this person had a strong need for love, affection and recognition. Might not this underlying need cause him—unconsciously or not—to choose many social activities from the cafeteria-line of life experiences rather than doing other things?

Might not many of his artistic activities—making unusual cards, growing pretty flowers, originating recipes, decorating his home in unique ways—also serve to bring about compliments from others, cause other people to like and appreciate him?

Of course!

But how many of us truly know what our strongest needs are? Have we thought much about how different activities can serve the same underlying need? Have we wondered about which needs of ours go together—fit—and form constellations or "need systems"?

Now I'm going to list many common needs and ask you to examine yourself objectively. Then I'll ask you to rank-order your main needs. Verify them with two people you trust—people who know you well. Then see if you can determine what patterns your different needs have already assumed, what your major need systems are.

Self Check List of Major Needs

belonging: a need to do things with others, to enjoy participating on teams, in groups, clubs, doing things together with others in cooperative relationships.

getting results: a need to be noticed, to be seen, to get positive attention.

conquest-victory: a need to win, to compete, to stand out, get ahead, to control, to lead, to be powerful.

psychological security: a need to be safe, to be protected, to feel your life is stable and predictable, to avoid tension and conflict.

structure: a need for logic and order, to have system and harmony in life, to synthesize experience, to bring order and harmony to your everyday life.

dominance: a need to have others listen to you, respect you, appreciate your ideas and actions.

helping: a need to grow and experience satisfaction by doing things which others see as being helpful, to play at assisting, giving aid.

conserving-holding: a need to maintain what you have, to save money, to exercise caution, to be sure, to check yourself and others.

81

social perceptiveness: a need to understand other people as well as yourself; a need to analyze social and political forces, to read your own motives and those of others.

social harmony: a need to get along well with others, to have them get along with you; to like others and be liked by them; to avoid stress and conflict.

independence: a need to make up your own mind, to "call the shots," to avoid being pressured or cajoled into action by others.

After reviewing these needs, copy the headings only on a fresh diary page entitled "Analysis of Major Needs." Then using the number one for "very strong," two for "moderately strong," three for "occasionally strong," four for "not strong," I would like you to rank-order each need on the list.

The person whose inventory assets we examined might demonstrate the following rank-order of his or her needs:

		Major Needs	*"Back-up" Needs*
belonging	2		
getting results	3		
recognition-attention	1		
conquest-victory	4		
psychological security	2	Recognition-attention	Belonging
structure	3		Psychological security
dominance	3	Social perceptiveness	
helping	2		Helping
conserving-holding	4	Social harmony	
social perceptiveness	1		
social harmony	1		
independence	3		

After you have rank-ordered each of your twelve needs, summarize all your number one (very strong)

82

needs under the heading "Major Needs," and under the heading "Back-up Needs" summarize all your number two (moderately strong) needs indicated in the illustration.

As a professional psychologist I've discovered that your major needs will typically give shape to your major behavioral choices in "fair weather conditions," in other words, when life is going along well. However, most of us, under conditions of stress or conflict, tend to revert to our back-up need system.

Thus, in the case of our socially and artistically oriented individual, he will vigorously pursue fulfillment of his need to gain attention, recognition and to make a powerful impact based on his creative behavior. However, under stress he feels flooded by the insecure feelings that gave birth to his recognition need and reverts to less ego-centered behavior. His lifestyle will, at least temporarily emphasize regaining a sense of belonging and of psychological security—and one good way of bringing this about is going out of his way to help others!

Knowing yourself and updating your self-awareness is hard work. I'm sure these exercises I've asked you to do in this chapter have seemed tough—and they were. They'll help you, however, to make sure your life is on the course of *your* choice, not someone else's. Millions of people waste energy because they don't know who they are or who they want to be. You're prepared now to be an exception. You've taken stock of yourself. You've made discoveries. Are you ready to translate them into behavior?

4. ARE YOU READY FOR AN EXCITING LIFT-OFF?

Self-Monitoring Tests That Evaluate Your Course

You've now been rigorously examining your previous lifestyle for approximately two weeks.

If you've kept up your diary and put into practice the suggestions I've made, you'll have a large reservoir of data about yourself. Now it's time to begin digesting it and using it toward increasing your personal effectiveness.

Let's summarize your first phase of self-exploration and see where you are:

1. You've made a serious contract with yourself to follow a systematic program of change. You've purchased and are using a self-development diary.
2. You're clearly aware that you are an energy system, that much of your vital energy has been wasted in the past.
3. You've analyzed your past pattern of energy loss via the "eleven deadly sins."
4. You've spelled out a series of specific actions you should take to guard against self-destructive energy applications.
5. You've performed an analysis of positive feedback and identified your strengths.
6. You've seen clearly the broad types of behaviors in which you excel.
7. You've looked underneath your behavior and begun to explore your essential behavior-shaping values.

8. You've been honest in recognizing the needs that make you tick.
9. You've formed some preliminary ideas which will be useful in predicting your own behavior under such unfavorable conditions as conflict or stress.

Congratulations! If you've seriously and carefully taken these nine basic steps of self-exploration, you probably have a more objective awareness of yourself than do most of your close friends and working associates.

You have more awareness of yourself than thousands of men and women who have paid literally hundreds of thousands of dollars to professional and quasi-professional counselors who promised their clients the moon and the stars and delivered almost no insight at all. But what are you going to do with this hard-won objective self-awareness? Forget about it? Leave it in your diary? Talk about it to impress your family and friends?

No! Not if you're as serious at recycling your lifestyle as I believe you are! You must use it! Daily! Otherwise you'll fail to bridge the gap between knowledge and action.

Remember this: *awareness is superficial if it isn't translated into behavior!* Behavior is the proving ground, the reality test, the laboratory in which you'll translate awareness into satisfaction. Think of your behavior during the next two weeks as a scientific experiment. A secret, unheralded, low-profile experiment which may nevertheless lift you to a new threshhold of being, feeling and doing.

Since your behavior will be experimental, I want you to "track" or record what happens to *you,* the subject of the experiment, as thoroughly and carefully as the human subject in a university experimental study. It will be necessary to log what happens to you each day, making in your diary the following observation entries:

Lift-off Readiness Log

1. Main things I did today:
2. What I enjoyed most:
3. What I enjoyed least:
4. Highest energy peak (log time of day/night)
5. Activity performed during EP (energy peak #4 above)
6. Leisure time use

Activity	Length of Time Performed
(list)	(list)

7. Vigorous physical activity
8. Relationship difference (see below)
9. (A) Deadly Sin of Energy Loss I Had to Wrestle With Today

   (B) How I handled It
10. Self-giving in response to someone else's need
11. Enjoyed activity which I overstressed
12. Things I regret having eaten or drunk
    (You must list specifics—excuses don't count —include the sweet roll this morning, that soggy sandwich, etc.)
13. Target thrust today On target_____Off target_____ (check one)
14. Tomorrow's must

The entries on this first page of specific self-monitoring should take no longer than ten minutes to enumerate but the revelations about yourself may literally save you months of otherwise wasted energy!

I'll show you how. But before doing so—an important caution. Remember my warning you to "make haste slowly" in recycling your lifestyle? Good. It is especially important that now you apply this concept to this portion of your recycling program. After your first day of lift-off, I want you to spend between twenty-four and forty-eight hours thinking and regrouping—reviewing your attitudinal commitment to the program. This should be a quiet, unhurried, reflective day or two. If the press of business or previously made social commitments prohibits this kind of peaceful self-reflection, then extend this hiatus of self-evaluation into the weekend or into a more tranquil weekday. Let's call this quiet time your *post lift-off guidance check and course modification*.

* Avoid excessive socializing during this period.
* Go back to basics.
* Ask yourself: How long have I been mastered, led, "victimized" by myself, my past pattern, my counter-productive habits?
* How long had you pondered reshaping your pattern of everyday living?
* Were you really serious about recycling your life-style? Are you still serious? More so?

Like many others who've launched into programs of self-development, you probably have the desire and, up until now anyway, a *generalized and serious commitment* to change and growth. So far, so good.

But wait. Did you perhaps swallow that italicized phrase too glibly? Think about it; reread the words: *generalized and serious commitment*. What does this mean?

It may mean that you're serious about self-development but went into it unwittingly hoping to "swallow the elephant whole!"

Maybe you thought too much in terms of an end-term desired result—the fine new you—and not enough in terms of *means*, the *processes* necessary to effect your improved lifestyle.

87

Let's draw a parallel to physical fitness. How many people have you known who seriously desired to become more fit, who got tough with themselves for a few days and then faded out and reverted to their previous habit patterns?

They probably didn't stop to:

(1) develop a *plan*
(2) determine if it was *realistic* and *right* for them
(3) how much time it would take over a *long term*
(4) how much time it would take on a *daily basis*
(5) how they would daily *monitor* their fitness
(6) what *criteria* they would use to assess change
(7) what *components* or *separate* physical *activities* might be desirable
(8) how they might *sequence* activities to *reinforce* the behavioral change desired
(9) whether the execution of their plan would provide *feelings of satisfaction*—whether it would be *fun*
(10) whether it would be wise to *design support* into the plan—do it with a friend or spouse

When you liftoff into a new lifestyle, what you're really doing is improving your *total fitness* as a human being! Recycling your lifestyle is not a fad or a project. It isn't a matter of sugarcoating everything you've been doing for the past few years.

Ideally, the person who's truly serious about recycling his lifestyle regards the process as continuous, infinite—in other words, as having no specific end-point in time.

Think of the world's beautiful people, not the jet-set pseudobeauties, but truly beautiful people: Schweitzer, Gandhi, Toscanini, Picasso, Einstein.

Consider the things they had in common:

(1) an unswerving commitment to develop their talents to the fullest

88

(2) a constant desire to experiment, to do new things

(3) the courage to be different, to withstand criticism, to recognize in the negative reactions of others positive confirmations of their growth and individuality

(4) the realization that giving freely of their talents to others would cause them to grow

(5) a precious cherishing of their energies and time

(6) patience and quiet tenacity, the conviction that long-term growth counts more than short-term instant impacts

(7) steady self-pacing and forebearance

(8) balance in daily activities; the ability to step back from themselves, to rest and "recharge"

(9) the willingness to smile and laugh, especially at themselves; perspective

(10) a fundamental underlying optimism, an ability to enjoy, to savor duress, frustration and denial as necessary ingredients in the process of self-development.

If you've thought through your commitment to recycling your lifestyle in specific terms and are willing to plan and monitor your lifestyle on a daily basis—using your diary and modifying your approach to each new day during the next two weeks, so much the better. If not, keep the faith. A few more days of planning, reading, thinking and reflecting will not be a waste of time. It may represent the best investment you've ever made!

As you re-evaluate the challenge of recycling your lifestyle, I'd like you to ponder several key points. I call them basic building blocks in self-growth. I'll list them now; during the next week we'll explore them in depth: *what* they might mean to you and *how* you can make them work for you.

1. Effective Time Management
2. The Need for Activity Analysis
3. Correlating Creative Work with EP's (energy peaks)
4. Improved Physical Fitness Aids Total Fitness
5. Controlling the Overstress of Enjoyed Activities
6. The Need for Daily Targets
7. Key Relationships Improve When You Make Initial Concessions
8. Self-Giving Means Growing; Generosity is a Habit, Not an Accident
9. Planning Tomorrow's Thrust

5. STRENGTHENING ATTITUDES, ELIMINATING BAD HABITS

Why You Should Think of Yourself in Different Terms

I have helped hundreds of men and women in industry to use psychoenergetics as the means of recycling their lifestyles. Not one of them has found it easy going. I think it would be useful if I shared with you the most common roadblocks that they've bumped up against—especially in the early stages—and how I've counseled them about overcoming these roadblocks.

Roadblock number one is the natural human tendency to think of lifestyle in terms of adding on a specific new activity to one's daily pattern of living.

If you've gotten into habits (as most people have) of wasting large amounts of psychic energy every day, taking up a musical instrument or registering for an evening college course won't suddenly enable you to productively utilize all your energies. You've got to think in terms of your *total* pattern of daily living.

Roadblock number two is the expectation of instant success.

In many ways, Americans thrive on panaceas. We're conditioned by the media that bombard us every day to think in terms of quick and easy formulas. We're conditioned to buy instant food and prepackaged cake mixes. We are sold three-day vacation packages at large hotels which promise (or at least, strongly imply) the probability of romance. Mail-order entrepreneurs hold forth a thousand "get rich quick" schemes. In short, we are being conditioned to admire instant success, ultra convenience and conformity.

Therefore, many men and women whom I have helped expressed disappointment after the first week or two of using psychoenergetics because they hadn't, within that short space of time, been able to see a melodramatic change in themselves.

If *you* expect such a change, you, too, will be disappointed. Recycling your lifestyle is going to take time. More importantly, it's going to take *discipline!* And discipline begins with the thinking process!

How many of us in the past have really been disciplined in our thinking? Now many, I can assure you. In the past few days, however, I've asked you to do some very serious, rigorous thinking. If you've followed my suggestions, you've been doing it. You've probably discovered that it isn't easy. An individual whose thoughts have been going down one conditioned track of thinking for thirty years doesn't switch onto another track overnight. If you've already faced up to this reality and are ready to come to grips with it, you've come a long way toward overcoming roadblock number two.

Roadblock number three involves irritation and impatience with the idea of keeping a diary about one's self.

There is hardly a man or woman I've helped to use psychoenergetics who hasn't complained about this aspect of the recycling process. Let me share with you some comments which clearly indicate roadblock number three:

"I'm a busy man, Dr. Mok. I just don't have time to keep a diary."

"The last time I ever used a diary was when I was eleven years old. I kept it up for a few months when I was a girl. What makes you think I'll be able to stick with the idea now?"

"The idea of writing down little things about myself is a waste of time. I don't see what good it will do."

"Writing all this stuff about yourself in a book is just a lot of mickey mouse as far as I'm concerned."

"I don't like it. It makes me feel very self-conscious. I just think it will take the spontaneity and fun out of living."

"The first few days I used the self-diary, I saw I was doing an awful lot of things I didn't like. I know it's going to be very depressing. Wasting so much energy is bad enough in itself, but when you force me to rub my nose in it you just make it worse."

"Okay, suppose I do write down a lot of things in my self-diary, what will it prove anyway?"

Most of these statements mean that the person in question has agreed that recycling his lifestyle is going to be difficult and that part of this difficulty will mean being more objective with himself—but when it gets down to the nitty-gritty, he's not so sure he wants to do it.

To my way of thinking, the above statements prove how truly important it is to keep your self-diary. It's one of the best ways to begin making sure that you're not kidding yourself. But there is more to it than that.

Let's take the issue of time. Honestly ask yourself, "How much time did I waste today just daydreaming? How much time did I waste today worrying?"

My studies indicate that most American men and women waste at least an average of three hours every day daydreaming and worrying. Let's suppose you daydream and worry less than the average—suppose you've only been spinning your wheels one hour a day.

I ask you to spend no more than ten minutes each day—and that's the maximum—making a few notes about yourself in the diary. I want you to take that ten minutes away from the sixty minutes you are already spending ineffectually on daydreams and needless worry. It's really that simple!

Another important reason for keeping a diary is that when an individual writes down something about himself, it tends to stick. It means more to him. He'll remember it. When you write down just a few words about something new and meaningful you really plan to do tomorrow, you increase the probability by tenfold that you'll accomplish that goal!

When a woman goes shopping, she makes a list of the groceries she needs. When she gets to the supermarket, she takes the list out of her pocketbook and checks it. If milk is on the list, she goes straight to the dairy case and gets the milk she needs. No wasting time or motion. Getting the shopping done is important to her and her family and doing it with the least amount of time and effort counts, so she takes the time to write it down.

Now consider for a moment how infinitely more important your lifestyle is to you than a daily shopping trip. If making a few notes on a daily basis in your self-diary will help you to recycle your lifestyle more effectively, isn't it worth doing?

Also, according to hundreds of men and women who have used psychoenergetics to recycle their lifestyles, their diary notations provide tangible evidence of self-change and growth. I believe you'll find this to be true for you, too. Try to get in the habit. If taking ten minutes late at night before you go to bed is something you find too difficult or onerous, then take only one minute. That's right, only sixty seconds to jot down in your diary the single most important thought or insight you've had about yourself that day. You'll be amazed, if you do this for a few months, how it will help give your lifestyle improved direction and meaning! Strengthening your attitude base—the underlying way you think about yourself and daily living—will proceed more smoothly if you employ what I call the ten basic building blocks.

Of the ten, one is so important—it's the foundation on which the other nine are built—that I call it the *super building block.*

The Super Basic Building Blocks: Remind Yourself of Basic Benefits!

That's the whole secret of developing and sustaining a new and improved set of attitudes about yourself and your lifestyle. It's incredibly simple, so much so that most people completely overlook it! On the other hand, I've discovered that when men and women do learn what it means and begin practicing it on a daily basis, it literally works wonders for them.

This is what I mean when I say: "Remind yourself of the basic benefits." Think for a moment how refreshing it will be not to be wasting huge hunks of vital energy on being afraid, on worrying needlessly, on assuming that you're going to fail before you start, on punishing yourself with guilt and recrimination. Think how exciting it will be to feel that you're in control of your own destiny, that you're doing the things you really want to do rather than merely reacting to the pressures imposed on you by others. Your sleep will improve. No longer will you toss and turn. You'll wake up in the morning feeling better, very likely even if you've had fewer hours of sleep than usual. You'll have more friends. You'll be achieving a sense of increased mastery, a heightened sense of inner peace. Aren't these some of the basic benefits we seek as we work toward recycling our lifestyles?

Of course they are!

The secret, then, is to remind yourself of these basic

benefits every day. They'll help you to regain perspective. They'll help you to reinforce your underlying commitment. They'll help you to make the daily use of psychoenergetics a reality.

Sure, you'll encounter frustration and disappointment along the way. That's to be expected. But one disappointing day doesn't have to mean defeat. When that difficult, frustrating, seemingly impossible day occurs, that's the time to use your secret building block. Come back to fundamentals. Remind yourself of what you're trying to accomplish and how worthwhile it really is. Remind yourself of some of the basic benefits you've already begun to achieve on preceding days. Recharge your psychic battery and do it often. The men and women most successful in making psychoenergetics work for them employ the secret building block several times each day!

They think about it early in the morning as they prepare to meet the challenges of the new day. When things unfold favorably during the day, they're likely to say to themselves, "I'm already seeing the basic benefits I sought—it's not a daydream, it's a reality. I feel more relaxed. I am enjoying myself and it really feels good!"

When they encounter frustration or disappointment—or begin to slip back on the old track of needless fear and worry, they remind themselves of the basic benefits. "Hey, wait a minute. That's the *old* me! Why should I give in? I have the capacity for inner strength. I've come a long way. I've gotten to know myself better. If I was able to achieve basic benefits on other days—and I know I have—I can do it today. Right now!"

Late at night, when the house is quiet, they make some notations in their diaries. They flip back to earlier pages and see their psychic growth unfolding before their eyes. They read and savor the basic benefits once more. They are recycling their lifestyles. It's not a dream, they're really doing it. Knowing this makes them feel good. Having thus reinforced themselves, they approach sleep in a relaxed and positive frame of mind.

Always remember your super basic building block! Ask yourself again: "Why did I start recycling my lifestyle? Where were the benefits I was really seeking?" When you have them in mind, ask yourself whether they're still important to you. Inevitably, you'll find they are. It's like flexing your muscles and feeling your own strength.

Now let's explore the other basic building blocks which you can employ to make those basic benefits happen!

A. *Effective Time Management*

All of us waste time. We know that, but we don't do anything about it because we think of time only as time. What is an hour—a morning or an afternoon? There're always more where they came from, right?

Wrong.

The reason such thinking is false is that when you waste time, you're wasting much, much more. What you're really doing is wasting vital human energy!

If you waste an hour worrying about something that happened years ago, something that can't be undone, you've wasted an hour's worth of energy that could have been used in growing. In learning. In social intercourse. In taking a pleasurable walk. In sharing experience with your children. In reading and extending your mental horizons. Think of all the fantastic other things you could have done with that energy.

But alas! That energy is gone. It's been wasted. What do you have to show for it? Nothing. And worse:

fatigue; poor digestion; an inefficient heart because of all the cigarettes you smoked during the many hours you wasted on worry. You have things to show for that misspent energy. But they're negative entries in the diary.

Begin thinking of time differently. Think of time as the stage on which the drama of energy unfolds. Think of time as representing opportunity. Think of time in terms of growth. Think of time not as something that is passing, but as a framework of energy utilization which *you can control!*

If you think of time in these terms, you'll want to explore how you're managing your time—if you don't, the very notion of time management will seem like a waste of time.

Please note that I say *time management* advisedly. Those individuals who utilize their own psychic energies most effectively are those individuals who manage time—not those whom time manages.

Your self-diary will show you more clearly how you are utilizing time and psychic energy. I've asked every man and woman I've ever helped to use psychoenergetics to make out a very detailed record or log of exactly what they did on a single typical day in their lives.

I invite you to do the same. Don't do it on a weekend and don't wait for a special day. Do it tomorrow or on any typical weekday in your life. Take approximately three sheets of lined paper and allow approximately four lines for each half hour of the day from the time you get up until the time you go to bed. Since we often forget by the end of a day what we did that morning, it usually works out best if you make your entries on the log at three or four checkpoints during the day. If you take a coffee break in the morning, spend several minutes logging in what you've already done since you got up in the morning. After lunch, update the log to include the things you've done since coffee. Do the same thing in mid-afternoon, and once again that night.

I have retained several thousand one-day time logs written on mimeographed forms I have distributed to corporate employees. There is a one paragraph empty space at the bottom of this daily log over which is printed the instruction: "Please Write Below Anything of Significance You've learned About Time, Yourself or the Utilization of Your Energies as a Result of Logging Your Time Today." The gamut of responses is amazing! Let me give you a few examples.

"I used to think I was working eight to ten hours a day. From the experience of logging what I specifically did during each half hour today, I realize I spent less than two hours each day working uninterruptedly. That's kind of scary!"

"I've realized the telephone is my enemy. I was on the telephone no less than twenty-three times today, and expended no less than one hour and forty-seven minutes on these calls. Only two of these conversations were actually necessary!"

"I spent three hours and fifty-two minutes today going back and forth between one place and another. It shocked me! I never before realized I make so many little trips to other people's offices, to the stationery store downstairs, to the coffee shop, to and from my boss's office. From now on I'm going to plan where I want to be and where I don't want to waste time going, and I know I'll have a lot more time to do the things that really count!"

"I didn't really get anything accomplished before eleven o'clock this morning. And unfortunately I have to admit today wasn't really an atypical day. I never realized all the little meaningless, mundane, repetitive and chit-chat things I was doing every morning. And I realized something else. The first three or four hours of my day are usually the hours when I feel best, when my physical energy is highest. In other words, I was using the best part of my day to do the dumbest things. From now on I'm going to concentrate on doing more important things as soon as I arrive at work. I asked a hotel manager to give me a "Do Not Disturb" sign and I've told the people I work with not to be surprised when they see it hanging outside my door in the morning. From now on I won't even answer the phone unless its an emergency. Thank you, Dr. Mok."

I am sure these insights don't surprise you. If they don't, chances are you're wasting your energy too. All the more reason, then, to pinpoint how. Once you identify the ways you typically waste valuable time and energy, you'll inevitably start developing strategies to prevent this needless waste. That brings us to the second building block.

B. *The Need for Activity Analysis*

Unfortunately, most of us proceed almost randomly through each day's experience—reacting to events and others' actions instead of deciding what our goals for that day are and then working out techniques to achieve those goals.

You don't have to be the hapless victim of circumstance and the whims of others. But you will be if you don't analyze your activities and take positive action based on such analysis.

It isn't hard to do at all. Your self-diary provides the perfect modus operandi. Assuming you have already logged just one typical day, all your activities will be listed right there in the diary in black and white. If you performed the exercise honestly—and if you behaved on that given day in typical fashion—you'll probably discover that more than fifty per cent of your time was

100

expended on activities that were unexpected, things that happened to you, burdens that were imposed upon you, interruptions in your schedule and so on.

If this is true, you will then ask yourself, "How come?"

Was it because these things were really so important either to the other people or to yourself? Or was it rather that you simply *found yourself doing them?*

The latter is much more common. Such occurrences will go on and on inexorably if you don't safeguard against them. Try envisioning what an ideal day would be. What activities would you plan if you really had a choice. Plot them out in your mind. Now remind yourself of this basic truth: *You really do have a choice!* You can make that ideal day happen!

It is essential to keep in mind that nobody else knows what you want to do—probably most people with whom you are interacting on a daily basis couldn't care less about your activities. Since they won't help you achieve this ideal day, it follows that you'll have to do it yourself.

Once you've mentally chosen the things you want to do on a given day, it logically follows that there will be many things you'll have to choose *not* to do. When your secretary lingers on the threshold and starts to tell you about the traffic jam she experienced on the way to work, you have a choice to make—right then and there: listen, or politely cut her short. It isn't necessary to be rude. You might say something like, "If I get back right now to finishing those reports, I think both of us will be able to leave a bit earlier tonight." Watch her smile and exit.

C. *Correlating Creative Work with EP's*

Each one of us has natural physical energy peaks—certain times within the day or evening when typically we feel best. These EP's are metabolic in nature and have recently received attention in various media. You've read about so-called *body time*. You already know whether you are a "morning person" or "night person."

Many professional individuals engaged in writing or scholarly research work best in the wee hours of the morning. My wife once told me, half facetiously, "Paul, if you weren't an insomniac, you'd probably never have written a book!"

The truth is, I've never suffered from insomnia. Many years ago, however, I discovered that I typically feel great in the middle of the night. If I had retired early, let's say at ten in the evening, I could wake up quite naturally at three in the morning feeling completely refreshed and at my best. Also, since I happen to be the father of four children, it didn't take me long to discover that if I wrote or engaged in research studies for three or four hours, let's say from three in the morning until six-thirty or seven when the others in my family would be awakening, I could work to my heart's content without a single interruption or distraction. Beautiful!

The point is simply this: I put my EP to work for me! Most people unfortunately do not. They fritter away their most precious energy peaks. How about you?

Have you stopped to consider your natural metabolic EP's? If not, start doing so at once. Make a few notations about these peak times in your self-diary. Choose a typical weekday and analyze very specifically, as you did with your log, precisely what you did during those three or four peak periods. You may discover that you wasted them all! Even if you spent only one or two EP's stargazing, reading a magazine or chit-chatting on the telephone, you've cheated yourself!

On countless occasions I've heard friends and acquaintances speak enviously about a well-known creative person. "He's so fortunate," the conversation goes, "to be so energetic. And to be so endowed with creative talent!"

But how fortunate is he? Is the man merely lucky? Is his success simply a question of native endowment? Hardly.

Every single one of us has the potential to create. Every one of us possesses more energy potential than he or she is utilizing. Frequently you'll find that the individual upon whom you look with envy has been endowed with no more talent than yourself. Physiologically he is no more energetic than you. What he has done in most cases, however, is to analyze his EP's and harness them! A large number of men and women who have applied psychoenergetics in daily living have reported to me that their friends and work associates were so impressed by the unleasing of new productivity that they attributed the cause to a new health food or patented medicine or dietary supplement my clients were thought to be using. "Where can I get it?" their friends asked.

The "it," of course, is in them too, but as I suggested earlier, the great majority of Americans expect to find life's secrets manufactured in bulk supply according to a formula. Start correlating the creative work you want to do with your EP's and watch the rumors fly!

D. *Improved Physical Fitness Aids Total Fitness*

If your daily habits do not promote health fitness, it will be difficult for you to recycle your lifestyle no matter how sincere and well intended you may be. If you eat and drink the wrong things, you'll know it and be wasting a lot of valuable time and energy worrying about how you look and how you feel. Your natural EP's will be blunted. You'll never feel great or really refreshed on any given day. It will simply be a question of when you feel less lousy. Clearly, such does not have to be the case!

Physical fitness doesn't require going to a gymnasium or health club but there are a few things it does mean. Let me list some of the basics:

1. The vast majority of middle-class Americans eat too much. No matter what you eat, cut down on caloric content. Particularly concentrate on cutting down on the amount of carbohydrates in your diet.

2. Eat fewer oily, greasy or fatty foods. Eat more fresh fruits and raw vegetables. Cut down on carbonated sodas and artificial juice-type drinks.

3. Walk up the stairs whenever possible.

4. If you live in the suburbs, sell your second car, buy a bike and ride to the railroad station.

5. On an everyday basis perform some *rigorous* physical activity with someone you like. In other words, enlist a partner and reinforce your efforts toward improving overall health fitness.

6. Go for the long pull, make physical activity part of your daily new lifestyle—something as important to you as the house you live in. Isn't your body the house your energy lives in?

7. If you smoke cigarettes, collect the butts from all the ashtrays in the house—all the butts which you and your spouse smoked—and deposit them in a gigantic ashtray in the living room. In two or three days it'll look like a small smoldering volcano. It will be ugly. It will stink. Disgusting! Leave it there, add to it daily. Stop by the huge smoldering mess and sniff it as you would fresh

spring flowers. Do you still feel like smoking? You may vomit—and you may stop smoking!

8. Run. Run hard whenever you can. It's the greatest exercise there is.

Many individuals who have practiced just these few daily health fitness basics have discovered that within a few weeks they feel more refreshed and more energetic in their non-EP periods than they previously did during their EP's! The human energy system constantly needs to be restored and recharged. Work *for* your energy system, not against it!

E. *Controlling the Overstress of Enjoyed Activities*

The woman who likes desserts will lose her battle of the bulge to chocolate eclairs. A man who enjoys vodka martinis will lose sight of the importance of his EP's via the cocktail route. Some of our worst enemies are not the things we fear or resent. They're the things we like most! Whatever a person does well, he may tend to do too much—possibly at the expense of developing other skills and talents. For example, an individual who is a good talker may tend to talk too much. He enjoys the impact of being regarded as scintillating. He likes the sound of his own voice, and clearly likes to know that others enjoy his repartee. In some cases, such an individual rarely finds time to crack a book. But time is clearly not his problem. His difficulty is letting go—relinquishing his over-use of his conversational skill.

The businessman who is very logical and enjoys clarifying problems which others cannot see so quickly, frequently tends to overexplain things.

The individual who is very neat and orderly finds himself telling his secretary time and time again exactly how to lay out each letter, what margins to use and so forth.

The woman who prides herself on her appearance may spend most of her time shopping for new and attractive garments. When she runs out of money or reaches the limit of her budget, she still goes to the stores and window shops. When she's not busily occupied in this activity, she finds herself poring over photo layouts of new fashions in the popular media.

Identify those activities which you are good at and obviously enjoy—pinpoint those things in which you may be overindulging. I am not for a moment suggesting that you *stop* doing these things. Rather, you should modulate or simply try to cut back as little as twenty per cent of the time you now spend each day using this particular interest or skill to the possible detriment of extending yourself into new activities—areas which are as yet untried.

F. *The Need for Daily Targets*

A man or woman without a goal is like a ship without a rudder. The goal-less individual will not achieve an improved lifestyle because he has never stopped to think seriously about where he is going or the kind of person he'd like to be.

But even when you have identified a few basic major goals for self-development, you have to go much further. The real test of recycling your lifestyle does not come at the end of a year or two—it comes on a daily basis!

The crucial tests of who you are, where you are going, who and what you are becoming—how you're approaching life, work and other people—are occurring each and every day. The fact that most men and women do not think of daily events as representing tests of themselves, is, in itself, part of the problem.

The sixth basic building block in recycling your lifestyle involves developing a particular major goal or target for yourself on a daily basis; planning how you'll insure achieving or approaching it; putting a game plan into action; then, stepping back late in the evening and evaluating, perhaps in your self-diary, how you've fared—how successful you were in staying on target, what you might have done differently.

You need not burden yourself with too many daily targets. Concentrate on just one—not necessarily a grandiose one. For example, your daily target might involve vigorous walking for twenty minutes, or spending one or two dollars less than you typically would on an average day, or allotting ten minutes of your lunch hour to serious meditation. Such activities, especially when extended and repeated, can assume great significance toward achieving behavioral patterns which provide increased satisfaction. Such daily targets are very simple and easy to achieve—but only if you set them for yourself and then deliberately steer yourself in a given direction!

G. *Key Relationships Improve When You Make Initial Concessions*

A certain degree of conflict with the key people in our lives is inevitable and, if handled well, a healthy thing. I'm not speaking of some melodramatic Hollywood version of conflict. A great deal of the conflicts which husbands and wives experience, for example, revolve less around major differences in social values than they do around simple, down-to-earth habit patterns. For example, the husband who enjoys reading is irritated by the wife who keeps reminding him to straighten out the disarray of books and papers on the floor. Conversely, the neat, action-oriented wife is irritated by the husband who always has his nose in a book.

The mother looks at her teenage son as someone

107

who can't stop talking. The teenage son who is told by his mother, "I'll think it over" sees her as a person who can't make up her mind! Whatever the problem of the moment, it's a natural human tendency to blame the other guy. *If only he'd be different. If only he'd see things differently. If only he'd be more like me.*

You're thinking this way about the other guy. The other guy is silently thinking the same things about you. Life and key relationships remain status quo, polarized as usual, each individual waiting for the other to move—to change—to show evidence of good faith! We are more than vaguely disappointed when the other individual does not make the first move. The basic secret for unfreezing relationships—for getting them out of a status quo mode—is so hugely simple and obvious, it's amazing that everyone doesn't see it and use it. If *you* do the unexpected, if you make the initial move, something interesting happens. The other individual does not stop whatever he's doing but something in his mind clicks almost out loud: he discovers you are not really the enemy after all, but someone who can be tolerant, understanding—a friend! He will be more relaxed, more accessible, more receptive to anything you wish to say or do. You may not succeed in bringing him around to your way of thinking that day, but no matter. You'll find if the other person likes you and values the relationship, he'll build on your initial gesture of good will and do something more consistent with your daily habit patterns or viewpoints. You'll have started a cycle of improved relating—something which might never have gotten off the ground if you hadn't made that vital first move!

H. *Self-Giving Means Growing* (Generosity is a habit, not an accident)

Sometimes I feel that the world would become

healthier if grownups followed the examples of children and if children learned to ignore, not imitate, their elders. Under normal circumstances most children enjoy social relationships characterized by a high degree of mutual trust and sharing. They give of themselves and to each other quite freely.

However, in the course of time many things happen which teach and condition them to become self-centered, grasping, socially isolated and mistrustful. As grownups, most of us walk around worrying about how the government, the landlord, the boss and the military/industrial complex are going to rip us off next. A man has little social territory he can identify as really being his own.

He clings to the tight little island of his family as he would to a battered raft in a hurricane. Small wonder that most of us are not very generous in our day-to-day behavior!

But if we were to increase our social territory, how would we go about it? What single thing could we say or do which would have the most far-reaching impact in getting others to trust us and reach out to us in a new, cooperative and friendly manner?

The answer is the building block which I call *self-giving*.

I use this term to differentiate the less personal kind of material giving, which is often thought of in materialistically-oriented societies as representing generosity, from the more meaningful concept of giving of one's self. How simple the concept, yet how many individuals do you see translating it into action on a daily basis?

Did you for only ten minutes today do something decent in response to the needs of another individual rather than in response to your own? Good. Assuming that you did, how did it feel to you? When the other person's eyes lit up, you probably completely forgot about yourself. This is one tiny example of what I think Emerson meant when he used the phrase a "transcendental moment." All of us unconsciously use and exploit those around us to our own ends. We're not only taking from others in terms of time; we are taking a toll in feelings. If we do nothing but withdraw—in terms of emotions—the investment runs out. There is no balance to show, the relationship fades away.

But if we begin making emotional deposits to others, if we give of our feelings—of our time and talents—we ourselves become rich because all of our social relationships become stronger. Just as selfishness is not an accident but rather a reflection of an habituated pattern, so, too, real generosity takes place because the giver makes it happen. He seeks to make it happen. He is thinking in terms of giving rather than taking and ripping off. How about you?

I. *Planning Tomorrow's Thrust*

Time and again we hear people say, "I never got off the ground today."

"I never really got going."

"I didn't really achieve any momentum until late in the afternoon, and then it was too late to make anything happen. Oh well. . . ."

As you recycle your lifestyle, each day should have a special thread—a special golden thread that weaves through the necessary, the disturbing, the trivial.

You are more likely to discover and extend that golden thread if you think about it, if you dedicate yourself to it. Cultivate the habit of building on new and emergent strengths. Maintain and extend the momentum of past success. It isn't necessary to wander into each new day like a man entering an unknown forest. First decide where you would like to go, what you would most like to see happen.

Would you like to cheer up those grouchy characters at work? What could you do to make them laugh? Are your children becoming television addicts? Would you rather see them learning to do a cartwheel or make something with their hands? What positive action might you take to make that happen? Is your husband or wife or someone you love going through a difficult period right now? Do they feel borne down, dispirited, overextended? Could they use a real lift—a renewed sense of support? What might you do to help that person? Let that thought become tomorrow's thrust! Remind yourself of it tomorrow morning. Commit yourself to making it happen—and you know something? It will!

PART TWO

PSYCHO-ENERGETICS FOR
BETTER RELATIONSHIPS

6. ARE YOU IN TOUCH . . . DO YOU RELATE TO YOURSELF

What Are Your Defenses, Your Distortions, Your Responses.

Are you in touch with yourself? To me, this question represents one of the most profound problems of our time.

America is the sum of its citizens. Our problems as a nation have not arisen simply because elected representatives are totally out of touch with the people they represent. Yes, our forms of government are outmoded and no longer work properly. But it is too simple to assume that all the destructive things America has done or allowed to happen represent the efforts of a small number of tyrants in Washington, D. C.

For many years millions of Americans have lost touch with themselves. They have lost touch with their fundamental humanity, with their ability to appreciate nature, with their sense of moral obligation to the poor and downtrodden, with their own self-respect.

Could it possibly be that these processes have affected only other people—that every reader of this book has himself or herself been immune from the malaise, from the pessimism, from the ugliness, from the destruction that has set in and caused moral and spiritual rot in our nation? No. I don't think so for a single moment. If I can be honest enough to admit to myself that many times—even as a professional psychologist—I had forgotten who and what I was, I can certainly entertain the possibility that at times you, the reader, have also been out of touch with yourself.

It's important for you to be able to limit that, to face the fact squarely. The person who cannot do this will go on like a naive child blaming others, will go on seeing himself as being "holier than thou." He will not grow. He will not change. The process of psychoenergetics is not for him. He will feel more secure playing the role of a small human windmill waving his arms frantically as he remains rooted to the same spot.

But we must now ask ourselves: for what reasons does a human being get too far away from his inner self?

Wearing a Turtle Shell Is Dangerous

Do you have a turtle shell? Of course you do. We all do. Our turtle shells represent our psychological defenses. We develop them in the first place to protect ourselves from being hurt, to shield our innermost vulnerabilities from outside attack. But the very shields we develop to ward off the attacks and hurts of others also serve to prevent the good things within ourselves from being outwardly expressed. How ironic that the barriers we develop for a positive and constructive purpose so often imprison us!

How Your Defenses Boomerang

Let's examine a few of the most common and frequently used psychological defenses—ones that you and I use every day perhaps without realizing it—and see how they boomerang.

Denial. This is a mechanism, a psychological trick we all use to keep our sensitivities intact, to lessen our awareness of pain.

116

Let us assume that you place your trust in another individual who betrays a confidence of yours to someone else. In truth, he has hurt you very much, especially because in order to acknowledge the seriousness of his wrong-doing it is necessary for you to acknowledge your own immaturity or error in judgment about his character. Rather than opening yourself to this possibility, you deny that what he did really bothered you that much. You say to yourself: "The confidence he betrayed wasn't really that important anyway." What happened in this instance was simply this: You used the common defense mechanism of denial to get out of touch with your own feelings.

Distortion. Each of us perceptually distorts in a direction necessary to uphold our most strongly held attitudes. Thus if we have been disappointed by others in the past and tend to be suspicious of those whom we don't know well, we will, in any given situation, immediately perceive the other individuals involved as trying to take advantage of us. We thus justify our social isolation, and muster all kinds of exaggerated evidence to prove the wrong-doing of the rest of the world. By distorting what we see and hear and by attributing false motives to others, we get farther and farther out of touch with the original building block of fear—our own feeling cornerstone on which the elaborate card castle is built.

For many, many years psychiatrists and psychoanalysts have had a field day taking their patients, over a period of years, through one defensive layer after another. Displacement, projection of guilt, withdrawal, fantasy wish fulfillment and so on. All of us use such mechanisms. All of us rationalize. All of us make excuses to conceal our feelings. One of the core problems, however, of traditional psychoanalytic practice (as it is still to this day being practiced) has been the

117

unproductive emphasis on explicating an individual's defensive mechanisms to him. Like a powerful and feelingless guide in an *Alice in Wonderland*-type story, the analyst helps the patient on an intellectual basis to see and interpret one Chinese mirror of defensiveness after another in his behavior and reactions.

This analytic practice is based on a gigantic but untested myth: namely, if the analyst is able to help the patient to understand his defensive behavior in intellectual terms, it will no longer be necessary for the patient to rely on these defenses—by some mystique he will suddenly spring free and behave differently.

Alas, every one of us can cite chapter and verse involving patients we know who, after years of such analytic therapies, did not spring free and indeed, who oftentimes became more adroit, devious and sophisticated in using the selfsame defenses to delude themselves, to remain out of touch with their own feelings.

However, even without the well-intended but negative effects of psychoanalysis, every so-called normal American man and woman is daily conditioned to conceal his own feelings from himself by the roles society expects him to play.

A forty-year-old father is rapping with his teenage son. For a fleeting instant, he is tempted to show feelings of irritation, of aggression, of empathy; he is tempted to show the still very much alive teenager within himself to his son so that the interaction can somehow come down to a more earthy plane. But he hesitates. He temporizes. Something within him says, in so many words: "Remember, you should behave as a father now."

He straightens his back in the chair, clears his throat, and makes a pronouncement. It sounds strained, superficial, pompous even to his own ears, let alone to those of his son. They remain at a distance.

The father complains to his wife, "It was no use. I was unable to reach him. He will not let me into his world."

His wife commiserates. As a mother, she has had the same experience. She knows her husband is right. She supports her husband emotionally, unconsciously reinforcing the travesty of the scenario. The father walks dejectedly back to the kitchen to get a highball. His wife retreats within herself. The father cannot see that in this brief but important dialogue with his son he was out of touch—not with the boy but with himself. If he could not acknowledge his own true feelings, how could he have expected his son to interact on the basis of his true feelings.

We are inhibited from acknowledging our feelings to the boss, to our subordinates, to our acquaintances—but most of all we fail to acknowledge our feelings to ourselves!

In order to recycle your lifestyle, it is necessary to begin relating to other human beings on a more down-to-earth, innocent, almost childlike basis. I would not say on a "natural" basis because the kind of interaction which would be desirable tends more to be the exception than the rule—tends to be seen as "unnatural"—and therefore "undesirable."

But it is impossible to relate to others in this way—in a truly open fashion, with spontaneity, with candor, without fear of consequences—if one constantly hides his feelings from himself.

The encounter movement of recent years has made one important contribution in the field of human communication: it has emphasized the acceptability of interacting on a feeling basis without knotty intellectual interplay. The advent of the science of body language and video tape instant replay have further enabled many men and women to see their physical movements

119

and behavioral styles contradict the words they are simultaneously speaking.

But it is not necessary to involve yourself in marathon therapy or encounter-group sessions or to rely on video tape methodology if you want to get closer together with yourself. There is a very simple but powerful technique which you and those closest to you can use as a means of getting back to what you are really feeling and what you are really trying to say.

I discovered this simple secret some years ago in communication role-playing sessions with managers and their subordinates. I designed these sessions so that individuals worked in groups of three. The "odd man out" acted as an observer who would tape record the role-play interaction between the other two individuals and take simultaneous observations on the dialogue, the unstated feelings, the nonverbal cues, the bodily movements of the participants—and then provide feedback data when the role play was complete.

Almost invariably the individual who was practicing a new communication technique would be shocked when confronted with the great storehouse of data on his own behavior which had been collected within only fifteen minutes. Initially, he would deny what he heard. Then his tape-recorded voice would be played back. When it stopped, he would blink, swallow hard and sheepishly admit, "Well, I guess I really was doing those things after all, wasn't I?"

After a couple of years I modified one of the observer data sheets and gave it to each manager, suggesting that he tape record a few role-play sessions and then a few live, "for real" dialogues with his workmates and then later, in the privacy of his own office, listen to the interaction and check it against a self-observation guide sheet.

The technique works marvelously! I was working

with one group of executives on a weekly basis and one autumn afternoon after we had finished a communications session one of the younger businessmen lingered after the others had gone. It was clear he wanted to speak to me privately.

"You know, Dr. Mok, while I've used these techniques to good advantage in my department, they've really paid off much more someplace else—at home."

He went on to explain that he and his wife had been having serious marital difficulties for almost two years and that when he had entered my course several weeks before, he and his wife had already contacted two separate lawyers to commence discussions about a separation agreement.

"But the funny thing that happened after our very first class," he related, "was that I started using these techniques with my wife. I guess I just did it unconsciously. I was so into the whole experience, I couldn't turn it off. She started to say things to me she had never said before. Our dialogue got into an entirely different plane. We were rapping with each other 'till two and three o'clock in the morning, getting to know each other better than I think we ever had—and that includes our honeymoon. I couldn't understand what was happening—or to put it another way, *why* it was happening. I asked my wife what she thought. 'How come we're suddenly not fighting with one another all the time—we made no decision to try to reconcile—how would you explain it?' Then she said it. 'Bill, what you've been doing in the last few days is something you've never done before. You're *monitoring* yourself!' "

The Secret Technique of Self-Monitoring

I truly hope that this young manager may some day read this book. More importantly, I hope it finds its

121

way into the hands of his wife, because it is to her, a person I never had the pleasure of meeting, that I owe this secret—this simple but tremendously powerful technique.

The moment Bill told me what his wife had said, something clicked in my brain. Of course! She was right—that was the secret. Role playing was no longer the issue. A third-party observer was no longer necessary. A self-observation guidesheet would hence forward be peripheral. If I could but teach every man and woman with whom I worked the importance of self-monitoring, and how to do it, what a magnificent breakthrough it could be!

The late Theodore Reik coined the phrase, "listening with the third ear." Although he used this wonderful phrase in a different context, it clearly indicates what I mean by self-monitoring. Most of us don't listen to ourselves and this is a tremendous and far-reaching problem. We very often make statements and express feelings to others—paying no attention to such data ourselves—and simply wait passively, perhaps only half listening, half perceiving the other person's response. It is difficult for us to deal effectively with the other person's data because we don't know what data he's reacting to. We've lost sight of our own input. *We did not monitor ourselves!*

Communication, using the secret of self-monitoring, is always difficult at first. The individuals, who, because of their professions, have usually become more practiced in the self-monitoring technique are actors and actresses—and to a somewhat lesser degree, at least in my personal experience, sales managers and politicians.

The actor is the best example. If he cannot gauge the impact of his words and gestures and alter them moment by moment, he is dead. He loses his audience and cannot regain it. Ask any actor who performs before a live audience. Every audience is different, every night he is doing different things—in the same role. In order to be good in his profession, he must constantly monitor himself—that is, listen to himself and modify as he goes along.

Now let's go back to the forty-year-old businessman father conversing with his teenage son. Imagine yourself for a moment to be that father. Only this time you're using the secret technique of self-monitoring.

Staring dejectedly beyond your son's face through the thin coils of smoke rising from some far-flung chimneys beyond the window, you hear yourself clearing your throat and then begin to speak. "Son, I don't think you really understand how your mother and I feel about some of the things you've been doing lately . . ."

Instantly your self-monitoring device swings into play. Why were you looking beyond your son? Avoiding the contact of his eyes? What about clearing your throat? What did this communicate to the boy? How about beginning the dialogue with the word "son"? How artificial this sounds, even to yourself! Why did you do it? What did it communicate to him? In that single instant you realize: *If I let myself continue the dialogue in this vein, we'll never get off the ground. It's I who have to modify, to make the first move. I must be able to show him that I can get out of my cardboard role and see myself in honest terms.*

Pull back. Stop. Take off your jacket and loosen your tie. Sit down. Begin fresh. "Jack, I think I was falling back on the pompous old father/son routine. If I start doing that again, let me know, won't you? I guess I've been worrying about having this conversation with you for two or three days now, and the tension must show."

123

Watch! Listen! The first thing you are likely to see is that your son changes the position of his body. His fingers loosen, his hands flop down to the sides of the chair. Now he sticks his legs out. His eyes stare at you critically, quizzically. On his lips is the flicker of a smile. "Well, yeah, Dad. I guess I know you were going to sock it to me sooner or later. I've been pretty tense ever since you said we ought to have this talk."

All of a sudden you are two human beings—two equally complex human souls getting in touch with feelings, breaking out of stereotyped role behaviors, each trying to understand the other.

How beautiful, how truly refreshing it would be if the majority of our conversations could function on this basis. But you can't legislate the process. You can't tell people to be open and expect it to happen instantly. You can't be like a sealed clam, hiding your own feelings within your shell and yet expecting other individuals to open up to you.

Practice the secret technique of self-monitoring. Don't be discouraged if people seem surprised or confused—and I am sure they will. There aren't many people walking around practicing it either on an intuitive or a learned basis and your new style may disarm others and may make them itchy, at least at first.

Let's return for a moment to the issue of underlying motives. It's important to recognize how different your motives will be from those of the actor, sales manager and politician who practice self-monitoring. These professionals use the technique in order to make certain strategic impacts on audiences, customers and voters. Clearly, they use self-monitoring as a means of screening out their own real feelings—as a means of not getting out of their roles, but of getting into them in a more adroit and sophisticated fashion.

The thrust of your self-monitoring will be precisely the opposite. Instead of filtering out your feelings and conveying a stereotyped role-bound impact on those with whom you have interacted on a daily basis, you'll practice self-monitoring as a means of getting back in touch with yourself—with your real feelings—and also as a means of enabling you to acknowledge these feelings to others.

One example of honest action is worth a thousand words of declaration. The real reason others will be itchy is that we are not accustomed to honesty. Therefore, view the disquieting reactions of others not as negative signals but as positive feedback indicating something different, something unusual and refreshing as happening between you.

If you communicate with the secret technique of self-monitoring, you'll discover that people giggle and laugh more. This will not be because what you are doing is essentially funny but rather "funny-strange." Think for a moment of the place where you work. Imagine your boss—or perhaps someone two or three levels above him in the organizational hierarchy—speaking to you about any given subject. Imagine the effect it would have on *you* if after a few minutes, he seemed to pull back out of himself, and said, "You know something? I didn't mean what I was saying just now. I really sounded like an ass—even to myself!"

You'd probably titter out loud. Wouldn't you? Wouldn't it be different? But remember, it wouldn't be bad.

There are several other things you can do which will help enable you to get back in touch with your feelings and which may also help those with whom you are interacting to get back in touch with theirs.

If Events Are Important, Bring to the Surface the Feelings That Surround Them

If you have one or more children who are now attending public school or who attended school in earlier years—think back to a typical conversation you had with your child about what happened at school.

"How was school today?"

"Oh, pretty good I guess."

"Did you get back any tests or homework assignments?"

"We got back the spelling tests from last week. I got an A."

"Is there anything bad that happened?"

"No, (hesitatingly) well, there was a fight."

"Were you in it?"

"No."

"That's good. Well, you better change your clothes now."

End of conversation. The parent's questions in this little scenario were strictly glued to the facts—to events. There is no mention of feelings. The parent gave the child no opportunity to express feelings.

Maybe the child wanted to tell how the "A" on the spelling test made him feel. Maybe the fight—albeit he wasn't physically involved in it—was very upsetting to him. Undoubtedly he had some feelings which might have surfaced. Maybe what was bothering him didn't have anything whatsoever to do with this event, but with some other happenings. But you never found out. You didn't enable him to get in touch with his own feelings. The conversation was mechanistic, stereotypical.

The Human Voice Is a Mask

One of the best ways you can monitor yourself and other people is by reading not their words, but the tone

126

of their voice. For example, suppose a friend is telling you about a crisis that occurred over the weekend. The individual was in a car accident, and he is relating how the car slid off the road and turned over, how the window softly cracked into a thousand tiny splinters, how bodies and handbags flew through the air, how the tow truck came and then the state police. And all the while his voice is a flat monotone. In other words, he is speaking with the same voice quality he would use to describe what items he had purchased for lunch that day in the cafeteria. Your monitoring device immediately picks up the discrepancy between the content and the tone being used to convey it. Clearly the voice quality is masking his real feelings.

It never ceases to amaze me how many individuals, in describing major crisis events in their lives, sound flat, as listless as if they were reading legal notices out of the Sunday Times. Nor are they typically the slightest bit aware of this discrepancy. If you tap into the probable feelings associated with the kind of events being described and give even the slightest indication of real interest, you'll find that the narrator's whole face and voice quality assume a different expression.

For example, with the friend describing the car accident—instead of waiting for him to betray signs of emotion—if you merely acknowledged the way *you thought he might have been feeling* by evidencing concern through your facial expression and saying, "My God, it must have been horrible!" chances are he'll lean forward, snap open his eyes, look at you as though he had been awakened from a dream, and say, "My God, it really was. For what seemed an incredibly long time—it was like a feeling of suspension of animation—I thought I was going to die. I remember thinking how ridiculous it was . . . and wondering whether

127

I had proper identification papers . . . and what would happen to the project I was supposed to lead on Monday . . . and only later did I think of my children, and then it was as though something caved in on my chest, and I felt nauseous as hell."

In other words, if you allow yourself not to be misled by the ordered and controlled tone and give him even the slightest jog in the direction of the way you think he may have been feeling, it suddenly becomes permissible and even a great relief for him to acknowledge his own feelings to himself and to you.

Even when your slight verbalization of the other person's assumed feelings is wrong, you'll usually end up in the right place. He'll animatedly contradict your trial balloon, the hypothesis in which you suggested the way he might have felt. For example, he'll say, "No. Wait. You don't understand. It wasn't that I was feeling horrible, it was more a question of helplessness. It was as though I were a tiny child—and everything was out of my control."

By the same token, as you practice self-monitoring, track your own voice. When you are trying to describe the joy experienced on a recent vacation, do you sound to yourself as though you are giving a canned chamber of commerce lecture? If so, don't be afraid to stop in midstream and stop ticking off place names, highway numbers, hours spent in different locations and other such statistical information your listener could glean out of a geography textbook. Get back in touch with the way you really felt that first morning when you woke up eagerly, as the dawn breeze bathed your relaxed body, and you walked out the red dry wood door onto the cool, lemon yellow sand and ambled down to the beach and watched a seagull skim effortlessly over the greenish clear water.

Recapturing the essential feeling will help you to re-

128

inforce the sense of tranquility and aliveness originally experienced. It will help you get back in touch with yourself. Also, you'll be giving more of yourself to the other person. Instead of merely conveying the outer shape, the skin of the orange, you'll be expressing some of the meat and the juice inside!

Suspend Judgments and Build on Positive Responses

One of the greatest roadblocks which separate your consciousness from your feelings is the tendency to make premature judgments.

Suppose you are trying to tell a friend about a really interesting learning experience you had at a business meeting sponsored by your company. Early in the conversation you preface what you are going to say as follows: "I know you'll think what I am going to tell you is pretty run-of-the-mill. I suppose these kinds of things, these human connections, are happening all the time at business meetings of various kinds, but the thing I wanted to tell you about happened this way . . ."

Chances are by that time you've already lost your friend's interest. More importantly, you've gotten out of touch with your own feelings.

Many of us irrationally anticipate the rejection of others. One way we unconsciously seek to cushion the effects of the anticipated turnoff is by turning ourselves off—by playing down or by making a self-critical negative prefatory remark before describing the event or the feelings that surround it. That way, if the other person conveyed the feelings, "That doesn't sound very interesting to me," you'd be protected. After all, didn't you start out by saying those kinds of things are probably happening all the time?

The irrational anticipation of rejection not only

cheats others, it cheats ourselves. It causes us to over-filter the communication of experience.

Why anticipate rejection anyway? Most people are so bored by their humdrum existences and so starved for more than an impersonal mechanistic recounting of facts and things, they'd be delighted to hear your honest expression of some real, flesh-and-blood human feeling.

The next time you start to filter your remarks or make judgments in advance about what you are about to say, check yourself. Use the secret self-monitoring device. Catch your breath and smile. Then say, "Hey wait a minute, I don't really mean that. I never heard of a connection like this being made at any business meeting. Now let me tell you what it was really like . . ."

By the same token, monitor your tendency to convey judgments about what the other guy is trying to say. Most of us don't do this either consciously or in obvious ways.

A friend is midway through describing a certain situation. As soon as he makes the first slightest pause, we interject, "But didn't you realize . . ."

Your friend will probably stop like a tightrope walker in midair, look distracted, let you finish the question, and then answer in a cursory fashion and quickly change the subject. You remind him he wasn't finished relating the situation. "Oh, well, it wasn't really important. The words, "But don't you. . . ." instantaneously conveyed a negative judgment, made him feel that you believe he shouldn't have done the very thing he was trying to have you understand.

If you would take notes on every conversation which you hear or participate in during a given day (I'm not suggesting that you do this although I have done it myself) you might be amazed to discover how few of our conversations contain the expression of any real feeling and how very very few are ever completed. Conversation in America usually represents an abortive and mutually tolerated exchange of basic information, fragmentary interludes that separate but do not link random but compulsive action.

It might seem initially futile to try to turn the tide on this cultural pattern of ours. But it's really not difficult at all. If you practice monitoring, tuning into your own feelings and others', observing nonverbal cues, listening for disparity between tone, voice quality and content, checking negative responses and judgments, you'll be rewarded by how much more meaningful the conversations you have with others will become!

There is another technique which is very simple and logical, although rarely practiced, which will enable you to bring out more feelings, more spirit and deeper levels of meaning in the conversations you have with others. The technique, called *Building on Positive Responses* was developed to a virtual science many years ago by marketing and advertising executives directing "think tank sessions" and "brainstorming" meetings.

These men, whose job it was to originate ideas for new products and product modifications, had discovered that when groups of people got together to discuss ideas, they usually criticized each other's contributions and therefore very little productive work came out. Therefore, they made an original basic rule that would apply to all brainstorming sessions—negatives, criticisms, are not allowed. However, this ground rule didn't take them far enough. In the absence of negative criticism, more positive ideas were generated, but they were going in all directions, there was no cohesiveness. The creative brains in the session were now each vying for the attention of everyone else.

Therefore, they took turns trying to see the viewpoint of one individual at a time, and everyone else in the room would join forces to help this individual (usually playing the role of the client for whom the product idea was being generated). This discovery reduced individual competition and increased cooperation.

Next, these men recognized the importance of extending an idea rather than abandoning it in midair. Thus, their next ground rule became, "Let's see if we can build on that idea!"

You can do the same thing without being in a brainstorming session. When you try to convey an idea, self-monitor yourself. Was that the best you could do? Did you convey the whole thing? Might there be extensions or other applications of the idea? See if you can build on your own ideas!

Support the other individual and help him to extend his ideas. Try to see what's good about his ideas—not what might be wrong with them. When you tell the other person, "Hank, let me see if I can build on your idea . . ." and then try to extend his thinking, you'll notice how cooperative he becomes and how much more freely he begins to discuss the way he really feels.

By building on his idea, you're conveying your respect for him, your interest in his thinking, your desire to know how he really feels and, perhaps most importantly, you are reinforcing him, building his ego. Believe me in this era of daily ego-assaults, feeling denials and negative judgments before the fact, anyone will find this *crediting* technique a truly refreshing experience!

7. INTERACTING, A TECHNIQUE FOR SUCCESS.

Inside the Communicative and Defensive Types

There is a very important distinction between purposeful self-isolation and the nonpurposeful negative feeling of loneliness. A lot of people fail to make this distinction, and as a result, they're most critical of their friends when they really ought to be proud of them!

The assistant editor who purposely uses her lunch hour to walk a mile to the park, linger at a health food store savoring a tall glass of fresh carrot juice and organically grown barley, and then walk the mile back to her office feeling exhilarated, healthy and energetic may be criticized by her workmates as being stuck-up, turning her back on the crowd, a snob because she refused to sit around the woman's lounge eating a greasy pastrami sandwich and potato chips and gossiping about the latest editorial intrigues!

This is a clear case in which the young woman in question was exercising deliberate, self-purposeful, positive isolation to recycle her lifestyle in a meaningful direction! For all that, her desire was probably not so much to be isolated, but to do her thing! Many times the young woman asks her workmates to make the two-mile walk and drink the carrot juice with her—but they have turned her down. They feel tired, their shoes are pinching, it's so much easier to have sandwiches sent up to the lounge!

On Friday afternoon following the end of the week sales meeting, a young sales representative joins his friend in the car pool for the ride out to the suburbs. The gang decides to stop at the local pub for a few beers and laughs over a game of shuffleboard—the twenty-five-cent adult version of the children's electric pinball machine. The young salesman in question says, "Thanks, but no thanks." *What's the matter with him?* the gang wonders aloud. *Is he so henpecked, perhaps, that he must hurry home to do the vacuuming for his wife?*

In fact, he has planned to go to the local Y and join one of his youngsters for a game of four-wall handball. After that they are going to take a swim. And after dinner he's planning to go down to his basement and continue puttering on the homemade sailfish he and his family are constructing for fun at the beach this summer!

"But Ralph, we just asked you to stop for a couple of beers, what's the big deal?"

The "big deal" to Ralph is lifestyle—cherishing each day, doing those things that represent optimal energy utilization, total fitness! He listens to a different drummer! He doesn't envision his plans as a "turn-off," a put down—a rejection of his friends.

They don't know where "he's at." They tease him. They use negative, derisive humor, trying to get him back on their track. He remains steadfast.

Ralph is not a "loner"—he's using healthy positive self-isolation to improve his lifestyle! More power to him!

Self-Isolation vs. Drifting

Contrast the above illustrations with these.

A young assistant editor has the "blues." Lunch hour is approaching, but she isn't particularly hungry.

134

She knows she can join her friends in the women's lounge. She can almost predict beforehand what lines the luncheon conversation will take. Somehow it seems so unproductive. She's heard it all before. Round and round, an eternal soap opera beginning and ending nowhere. The idea turns her off. But she has no particular alternative in mind. She decides to do some extra work. She remains at her desk and then does some filing. Twenty minutes of her lunch hour slides by. Suddenly she realizes that if she keeps puttering away, the lunch hour will vanish. She feels tired, dispirited. Maybe it would be nice to take a walk. She looks out the window. It is gray outside. She looks back at the clock. It is now 12:25. Not enough time really. She wanders out of the office, takes the elevator and goes alone to a crowded coffee shop. Like a sleepwalker in a vague and meaningless dream, she orders the quickest and cheapest thing—a frankfurter, french fries and a regular coffee. The food is greasy, unattractive; she nibbles, plays with it, then pushes it away. She lights a cigarette. She walks outside and aimlessly meanders down the street. She window-shops in front of one of the boutiques. She goes next door into a stationery store and considers buying two cards. She looks at her watch. She decides she doesn't need them now. She goes back upstairs, wondering what her friends are doing. She stops into the women's lounge, where an animated conversation is in progress. She listens a bit, reacts passively, smokes another cigarette, then leaves. Back to her desk. Randomly she picks up a stack of interoffice communications. She looks at the clock. Four more dreary hours to go. How will she get through the afternoon? She feels so listless. Vaguely depressed— she isn't sure why. She hopes one of her friends will call her this afternoon.

Later on the same Friday afternoon after the sales

meeting is finished, the gang goes out to the parking lot, the car maneuvers slowly through the growing weekend rush-hour traffic. The guys are still bantering animatedly about Hawkins, the sales manager, about the overhead projector that didn't work, the look of embarrassment on Hawkins' face. Ralph is bored. For the umpteenth time, the other guys are shooting down Hawkins. Ralph is vaguely angry. Just one time he would like to rear back on his hind legs and holler, "Now what in the name of God is really wrong with Hawkins—isn't he a human being? Really trying to do his job? If he goofs, shouldn't we help him? What's wrong with us, guys? Are we just a bunch of babies, always looking for the easy way out—blaming big daddy? Could we have run the meeting that much better? If we could have, why didn't we volunteer to do it?"

Oh well. It isn't that much of a big deal. I guess, Ralph thinks, *If I were such a hotshot, I would have done something different. Who am I to criticize?*

Someone suggests stopping at the local pub to have a few beers and laughs over the electric shuffleboard game. The week before, the guys did exactly the same thing. Life seems so predictable. So God-awful institutionalized!

What's wrong with *me*, Ralph wonders. Clearly he feels alienated—and *guilty!* He doesn't know why, but he's convinced: something must be wrong with him!

Although he doesn't feel much like going to the pub, he doesn't have anything else planned. So he keeps his mouth shut and goes along with the program.

After a couple of beers and the tick-tack-tick of several shuffleboard games and the usual light banter with the bartender about the professional big league games scheduled for the weekend, a couple of his friends switch to martinis and begin a more serious rap session. Real hostility emerges in their discussion of the sales force, the recent reorganization of the territories, their boss, Hawkins, and all the various and sundry injustices of the travel schedules and the new commission structure. Ralph looks at his watch, mentally checks his wallet and decides he'd better be moving on. He makes his excuses. Someone complains. "What's the big deal, Ralph? Worried about the tab? We can expense it. You're not going to turn us in, are you? Ha, ha. . . ."

He doesn't want to be cast in the role of Johnny Good-Good, the group conscience. What the hell. He decides to stay for one vodka martini on the rocks. His mind drifts. He half-tracks the conversation. Finally he manages to squeeze out of the booth, makes his apologies once again and leaves. "Ralph has to get home and finish the ironing before his wife gets back from her mahjong game," someone says. "Ha, ha." Just one time he'd like to take Frank, the guy who just made the ironing remark, and punch him right out.

Ridiculous, he thinks. *What the hell is wrong with me, anyway?*

He takes the bus, walks the remaining two blocks to his house and enters. No one is home. The kids must be out playing. His wife must be shopping. He checks the mail—more bills. How is he going to make it through the month?

He'd like to take the family out to dinner, but who can afford it? Maybe he and his wife will just go to a movie. Can they afford that? Is it really worth getting a babysitter?

He washes, changes his clothes, takes some papers out of his briefcase and scans them listlessly, then puts them back. He goes to the bedroom and lies down. What to do? He glances at the phone. He feels like talking with someone, but he doesn't know who. If he did call one of his friends, what would he say? He really doesn't have anything specific in mind. He glances at his watch. His wife should be home by now. Why isn't she home? Why hasn't she started making dinner? He isn't hungry, but he is aware of his resentment toward his wife. He picks up the *TV Guide,* and glances at Friday's schedule. Kiddy programs and then the evening news. He checks the schedule for later, looking for a good movie. Too bad, only serial reruns. He goes to the kitchen and pours himself a really strong drink. He realizes he's drinking too quickly, but does so anyway so that he can manage perhaps two more stiff ones before the troops return. He takes his drink and the vodka bottle back to the bedroom, kicks off his shoes, lies down, props up his head and shoulders on several pillows and stares at the ceiling. He returns to the self-dialogue of recent weeks and months.

What's wrong with me anyway? Why is life passing me by? Why don't I feel content? Am I getting old before my time?

Soon his kids will be back, making noise and hassling each other. Probably he will snap at them. Then Anne will return, and take the kids in hand. "Can't you see your father is tired? You must realize he's had a very hard week at the office. Let's let your father rest. Now be quiet and go watch television, and be sure to close the door."

Boredom Is a Learned Behavior Pattern. Start Unlearning It Today!

Boredom—and its inseparable companions, listlessness, fatigue, drifting, passivity and depression—is a major plague of our time!

Boredom never represents a single situational occurrence. If that's the way you've thought of boredom before, you've been kidding yourself. Boredom is a much more serious, long-term process, based on a certain type of thinking, a sequenced pattern of behavior that is built progressively, albeit unconsciously, on this certain special, self-destructive way of thinking.

The nonproductive lifestyle of boredom is based on nothing more nor less than *dependent thinking!*

But where does this dependent thinking come from? How does it start—and how does it set in?

Typically it starts in childhood, sets in during the adolescent years, is overlayed and masked during early adulthood, then reasserts itself as a serious, prolonged pattern in the late twenties.

Think back to a time in your preteenage years. "Mommy, what can I do today?"

It is right then and there—not only in the child's question—but in the parent's typical mode of response to it—that boredom begins to set in. If we as parents make the mistake of programming our children's activities, telling them what to do so that they will not be bored, we only help them to become more bored, more dependent on us and the things we tell them to do to escape the feeling of loneliness.

Imagine for a moment that every time a youngster asked his mother or father what he should do to alleviate boredom, one of his parents gave him movie money, told him to watch television, bought him a new toy or, in any way your imagination suggests, *assumed responsibility for the child's distraction*. What would be the consequence? Instead of growing up as a self-directed, independently oriented young person, the child would remain an emotional infant, inevitably criticizing others—his friends, his wife, his boss, his workmates, the town fathers and the current federal administration in power—for not providing him with more stimulation, more fun, more meaning in his life!

Believe me, there are literally millions of Americans—adults in years but psychologically still children—who are doing precisely this!

For years this felony has been compounded by four-year liberal arts colleges which have reinforced this unproductive way of thinking, which have forced this dependency to feed on itself rather than breaking the cycle! The institutions of orientation weeks, activity clubs, fraternities and sororities, competitive team sports, etc.—programs designed and fostered with all good and sincere intent—have made many of our colleges into nothing more nor less than extended kindergartens which breed and nurture dependency which, in turn, breeds boredom.

However, millions of adult Americans have been so brainwashed—and I use the term advisedly—that instead of looking back upon their college years in a spirit of critical and constructive anger, they view the four lost years of their outerdirected passivity with a saccharine nostalgia, sadly wondering why their suburban cooperative can't be as much fun as the group sings, prep rallies and sorority milk-punch costume parties of those halcyon, carefree, responsibility-free days!

To be sure, the college scene is changing, but there is an entire generation of Americans who attended college prior to the marked shift in our colleges toward increased independent study, community involvement and work-study programs and away from calcified and irrelevant curricula, canned lecture courses and learning by rote.

Nostalgia is unproductive, destructive! To the extent that you fall back into this way of thinking, check yourself. Self-monitor!

Reorient yourself! Don't be disappointed and critical of those you love, those you work with! When you allow yourself to think this way, you're unconsciously falling back into the dependency orientation! Without actually saying so, what you're really complaining about is that others are not taking care of you, are not providing distraction and fun things and meaning. Now isn't that an unrealistic, unhealthy, childlike expectation?

The individual who is using psychoenergetics to recycle his lifestyle is never bored! He begins by declaring to himself: "I am an adult!" He repeats it to himself, reminds himself what it means! It means: *I am independent, I think for myself, I do not expect others to solve my problems. I can control my destiny, I do control my actions, I am what I do, I do what I think. I must think for myself, I will think for myself, I have no reason to feel sorry for myself!*

In order to conquer the feeling of being bored and the experience of boredom, it is initially necessary to go back to your secret building block, to remind yourself of the benefits of self-reliance!

Self-monitor yourself! When you begin drifting, check yourself. *What do I really want to do right now? What would really be fun? What would really be productive?* Then do it!

I think you can see now how your self-diary can truly help you avoid the learned boredom pattern. If the assistant editor and Ralph, the salesman, had used their self-diaries last night to plan out their major thrusts for tomorrow—if they had performed a daily log and activity analysis—they would have seen, before the fact, pitfalls of a drifting lunch hour and a random, outer-directed afternoon! They would have safeguarded against being trapped into nonproductivity by outer-directed others! As in my earlier illustrations, the assistant editor would have planned to use her lunch hour in a healthy, productive and constructive way, as

Ralph would have planned before the fact to play handball and work with his family on the summer sailfish! If you don't control your thinking prior to experience, your probabilities for doing healthy constructive actions at any given time are geometrically reduced!

Get in the habit of anticipating! Of planning! Of self-monitoring! Of acting out your self-reliant plan! Of evaluating your success! Of self-reinforcement!

Use Self-Picturing to Handle Conflicts Before They Occur

Many years ago I found myself being constantly brought up short by men and women whom I was trying to help use psychoenergetics to improve their daily patterns of living. In one form or another, many of them would tell me, "The problem, Dr. Mok, is that I get sucked into things. I go along for a few hours following my daily action plan and everything's okay. Then, whammo! Somebody throws me a curve ball. Some situation occurs that I didn't bargain on, and before I know it, I'm right in the middle of it. Trapped! After the fact, I realize that the situation was unproductive, that I wasn't able to help the others and that I certainly didn't help myself. But the problem was, I couldn't avoid it. So many things happen that I can't bargain on—these are the things that upset my efforts to use psychoenergetics. You know, 'The best laid plans of mice and men . . .' It's not that I don't believe in psychoenergetics or think it isn't a good process . . . It's just that so many other people, critical outsiders, aren't with the program—and they couldn't care less!"

I recognized this, and still do, as a very valid problem. But it's not an insurmountable one. I came to realize that if a great many of the typical conflict situations an individual found himself in came as "curve balls," or surprises, and if the individual had not been forewarned and forearmed, there'd be no reason to expect that he wouldn't be sucked into these situations! The problem, then, was how to anticipate the unanticipated, how to "read" the curve ball before it was even pitched, how to bargain for the surprise so that when it came it wouldn't be a surprise at all!

After pondering this problem, I finally developed a method which I used to call *conflict insurance*. It worked quite simply. I simply asked the managers with whom I was working to list on a piece of paper all those specific situations occurring during the past two weeks in which they had felt "sucked in" or helpless. I asked them to specifically document the critical *others*—bosses, subordinates, husbands, wives, friends or colleagues—who typically (i.e., with the highest degree of frequency) were the ones who had initiated these disturbing situations or events.

It soon became apparent to the managers that these behavioral traps really could be anticipated since the flak not only assumed certain predictable forms, it usually also typically came from one or two main "curve ball pitchers."

At about this time in my industrial and management consulting experience I became quite intrigued by a management strategy developed by my psychologist colleague, Dr. John Flanagan. He called the strategy the *critical incident technique*.

He used the strategy at General Motors, for example, to help foremen and department heads to identify, from specific histories of past experience, those situations which had had the most negative effects on production and quality. After carefully reviewing such situations and by prioritizing them according to frequency of occurrence and severity of effect, he was able to help supervisors to know beforehand what situations represented "critical incidents." Then he worked with the supervisors to develop techniques and methods—before the fact—which would enable them to handle these critical incidents more effectively.

In later years, a number of Dr. Flanagan's associates, including, for example, Grace Fivars, extended the critical incident strategy as an institutional training device. Miss Fivars brought the critical incident strategy into hospitals all around the nation, using it with nurses to identify what situations were most disturbing in terms of total patient care. Enumeration and analysis of the situational data enabled the nurses to pinpoint the fact that much of the trouble was due to the lack of ability on the part of student nurses *to anticipate and deal effectively with unscheduled, unexpected critical situations* involving patients. Once such critical incidents were properly identified, Miss Fivars worked with those on the hospital staffs responsible for nursing education to (1) make sure that such critical incidents were thoroughly understood by student nurses in their regular training, and (2) explore methods and techniques for handling such critical incidents more effectively.

In those hospitals and manufacturing companies where the strategy has been used, production and patient care have markedly improved! Fewer "curve ball situations" seem to occur. Newly promoted supervisors, foremen and even student nurses are handling difficult situations more competently! The ability of such individuals under stress or in the face of crisis to maintain their composure, to think logically and analytically, and to make fast and effective judgments has considerably improved.

Now let's put you in the driver's seat. I don't think it

would be difficult for you to pinpoint quite accurately the kind of situations which typically result in conflict, wasted time, frustration and wheel-spinning for *you*. Nor do I think that you would find it difficult to trace back the source of such flak and pinpoint the one or two individuals who (perhaps because of their own personalities or their own inabilities to handle conflict effectively) unwittingly cause you to feel trapped in these hassling situations.

But if that's as far as you went, you'd still probably find yourself in considerable difficulty. You'd probably wind up writing down in your self-diary something like this: "I figured that most flak would occur at work in the last three days of the month when we got ready to do the budget report and sure enough, it happened! I thought the trouble would start with Jenkins, the boss, throwing a temper tantrum and asking me to stay overtime, and sure enough he did! I figured I'd probably have difficulty on the weekend when my husband would insist we go out for pizza and that I should take the children off his back on Saturday and Sunday and sure enough, that's what happened!

Clearly, the missing ingredient is the most vital one—the action plan or techniques which you would use to handle these predictable trap situations!

On a group basis in a work situation the methods explored and agreed upon for handling conflict or critical incidents typically involve a group or team approach. That way one individual doesn't have to fight the flak alone. He or she has the previously-agreed-upon frame of reference to revert to, to call attention to as a means of gaining support in managing the conflict.

As a lone individual trying to recycle your lifestyle perhaps without the support, understanding or sympathy of critical others around you, your situation is dif-

145

ferent—more difficult. Granted. What can you do? You can use the technique of *self-picturing!* It works like this. You have clearly anticipated that the flak will occur around the monthly budget report time. You have clearly been able to anticipate, on the basis of past actions, how Jenkins, the boss, will handle himself and try to interact with you the next time.

At home late in the evening when all is quiet, clearly *picture* various things which you might say to Jenkins before the fact. Try to picture, or envision, different options. Picture how it might be if you approached him two or three weeks before the monthly report—on what I call a fair weather day, when he is relaxed and composed—and discussed with him a way of avoiding the typical eleventh hour end-of-month crisis. Picture to yourself how it might be if you spoke with two or three key workmates and arranged with them a method for reducing the confusion and integrating your mutual efforts more effectively. Picture what might happen if the boss rejected your initial suggestion. Picture what it might be like if you, once having gained the support of three workmates, asked the boss if he could join the four of you for a prework early morning meeting to explore an improved team approach to this group problem situation.

Picture in your own mind how you might approach your husband—not at the last minute when he is already mentally committed to having the family go out for pizza, but earlier in the week when he is relaxed and composed. Picture what it might be like if you initiated a conversation with him about the ways the family typically spends the weekend. Picture the scene not as an argument, not as an attack or a negative judgment on him, but rather as a mutual effort aimed at improving family lifestyle! Picture your own response in the face of his initial bewilderment, or rejec-

146

tion of your first idea! Do you picture yourself becoming angry, feeling hurt?

How would feeling this way, and showing it, affect the process of interaction? Picture yourself self-monitoring!

Picture yourself listening better, letting your husband air some of his grievances, some things he feels you don't understand!

Picture the possibility of modifying your own action plan. Picture his possible response to your suggestion that he and the children go for pizza and perhaps extend their time together in a mutually enjoyed activity such as bowling. Picture the things you might do if you had four hours just to yourself!

Picture yourself compromising on a way you and the children, by working together as a team, could accomplish more household chores on Saturday morning, and permit your husband to remain in bed asleep several extra hours! Picture his response to this suggestion. Picture your next steps!

Time and again I am pleased and gratified to discover that those men and women who are greatly admired for their relaxed and seemingly unflappable cool in the face of crisis or conflict are no different from you and me! That they are not born with ice water in their veins—or a nervous system that is different in any way from yours or mine. Inevitably, discussion with these people has revealed that they have been able to picture beforehand what's likely to happen, who it's likely to happen with, and how they themselves are going to respond and handle themselves and the situation.

Many so-called supersalesmen in industry have confided to me that the technique of *self-picturing* represented a major turning point in their careers!

How many times in one form or another have I heard this story: "I'll never forget, Dr. Mok, the time I had a rare opportunity to introduce a new system—totally on my own—to a major account. I burned the midnight oil reviewing down to the finest detail the customer's organization—his problems, his people and his practices. I knew my system would work. I knew it would help him. I knew I had the answers. I rehearsed my presentation beforehand. I ironed out the wrinkles. When I went in to see him, I looked good and felt good, I was confident. Then it happened! From out of nowhere he threw a curve ball—and I blew my cool. I became threatened and showed it. I didn't want to argue with him, but before I knew it, I was telling him chapter and verse of how hard I had worked on the new system, how much it meant to me to get his business—I was acting like a hurt child, trying to get him to feel sorry for me—and getting deeper in the hole in the process. It was only later during our conflict management discussion that I realized I really hadn't done my homework after all. I had failed to picture that very critical possibility. If I had pictured it and had pictured four or five optional responses and had worked these through clearly in my own mind, I never would have experienced panic—I wouldn't have had to grasp for straws. And something else. You helped me to picture what it would be like in that situation when, even after doing my self-picturing homework, an unexpected hard curve ball came in. One I had tried to picture but couldn't. I learned to picture myself remaining composed and confident even when I didn't feel that way. I was able to picture myself remaining cool, continuing to listen and explore, buying time to *repicture* during the crisis itself. I can honestly say that during the past three years by using this process of self-picturing, I've probably been able to eliminate eighty percent of those situations which might have been unexpected and upsetting in the past. And by re-self-picturing, I think I've been much more effective in handling the remaining twenty percent!"

Suppose My Productive Self-Isolation Conflicts With His?

This question is among the most important you'll have to come to grips with in the course of recycling your lifestyle! All of us—regardless of age, sex and specific family status—are interacting daily with key others. Can we assume that our more rigorous efforts to do these things which are most important to us, to be more self-disciplined, purposeful and directional in the way we approach life and work will be easily understood and appreciated? That they will make no waves? That these key others will necessarily emphathize and be receptive?

Of course not!

Prepare yourself and picture it. If there were no particular visible signs of conflict in your relationships before, the more successful you become in recycling your lifestyle, the more previously veiled conflicts are likely to surface!

An individual who is successfully recycling his lifestyle on a daily basis is not an easy person to live with! By very definition, he can't be. If he were to completely give himself over to the needs, wishes and pressures of those around him, if he surrendered his daily thrust or sense of purposefulness in the face of the least and first setback, how successful could he be?

Add to this the very real possibility that those key others in your daily interaction patterns may be trying to recycle their own lifestyles! Is it not more than vaguely possible that the things which you regard as unswerving commitments of your own represent—or

149

could represent—impositions, denials, self-centered activities in the eyes of a key other?

Of course it's more than vaguely possible. It's inevitable! And that's why the process I call *linking* has vital significance. There are two basic aspects or components to the process. They are as follows:

A. *Establishing Informal Contracts*

Suppose you're a busy housewife with two preschool children and a hard-working, ambitious husband. Let's assume that you had launched into a vigorous effort to recycle your lifestyle—and said nothing whatsoever about it to your husband. You would then have been working in what I call a *self-vacuum*. Picture what it would be like under such conditions if you committed yourself to vigorous three-mile bicycling three mornings a week, let's say every Monday, Wednesday and Friday.

Monday morning. Seven o'clock. The alarm rings. You leap out of bed, shower and dress in your old blue jeans and Beethoven sweatshirt. Your husband half-awakens. "Where the heck are you going?"

"On my three-mile, vigorous, total-fitness bicycle jaunt, of course!"

Need I say more? Your husband would think you had slipped a mental disc, the children would be screaming, and next thing you know, there'd be a battle royal!

Thus, if you're married and have a family, it's very important to enlist their understanding and cooperation in what you are trying to do and, at the same time, assure them of your flexibility, cooperation, understanding and support!

I see this as a difficult and evolutionary process, not a single, magic conference.

Certain ground rules or guidelines have to be established. These constitute the basis of what I call your *informal contracts*.

First of all, employ a maximum consideration of others in establishing your activity schedules. Try to arrange to have your cake and eat it too! If your husband is not already involved with the concept of recycling lifestyle, try to make him a partner in the process. If he isn't ready, in a quiet and composed way, try to help him see not only the benefits for you, but the basic benefits to him as you look better, feel better, accomplish more and grow!

Head off controversy and conflict before the fact by getting him to agree on certain key aspects of your proposed activity schedule. These are action musts! If he can be brought into such activities and enjoy and benefit from them, so much the better. If not, explore the possibility of making a trade-off with one of your neighbors or friends. Perhaps another woman your age with a couple of preschool children is willing to engage your children and her own in a constructive activity later in the morning when you go cycling; perhaps in the afternoon you can lead an activity involving your children and hers while she plays tennis! Now you have an ongoing informal contract with a friend and now you also have the basis for a viable informal contract with your husband!

No curve balls, no surprises, no situational conflict! By developing, maintaining and safeguarding such informal contracts or agreements, you initiate the vital process of *linking* the actualization of your needs with those of key others in your life!

B. *Situational Linking*

Once you've made the basic informal contracts necessary to engage in self-disciplined purposeful activities within a framework of cooperation and under-standing, you'll find that things proceed more smoothly. Sure, there'll be raised eyebrows, some teasing and some grousing along the way. But you've anticipated that and, by self-picturing your responses, have probably been able to handle the garden-variety flak more effectively.

However, as you hang in there, committed to the endurance aspect of recycling your lifestyle over the long term, what's likely to happen? Your neighbor friend with whom you have the trade-off arrangement has to move. Your husband becomes ill. One of your children becomes moody or difficult for no apparent reason.

If you were an extremist—or if you were totally unprepared mentally for such occurrences—you might react in either one of two main immature ways. The first would be to become so up-tight and rigid in the face of the unexpected that you would unconsciously divorce yourself almost completely from the needs of others—your husband, your children, your friend, the world! You would force yourself to stick to your schedule on that given day at that given time, come hell or high water!

Or, conversely, you might simply scrap altogether your efforts to recycle your lifestyle! You could cop out. You could rationalize it by telling yourself, "I knew it wouldn't work—it's too difficult, why even bother to try!"

Neither response pattern would be constructive. Both extremes can and should be avoided. The technique which will enable you to remain flexible, responsive and still basically on target is what I call *situational linking*. This process begins by developing a mental set which I describe as "reasonable flexibility." You recognize on the one hand that it's almost impossible to draw the line between extreme flexibility and wishy-washy passivity. On the other hand, you also recognize that extreme rigidity results in selfishness and an inability to respond effectively to the needs of key others. That's why it's necessary for each of us to develop a viable midpoint in his own mind, a midpoint of reasonable flexibility.

While you recognize that on a given day it will just be physically impossible for you to engage in an important, preplanned activity, you can still remain firmly committed to the thrust and to your long-term commitments.

More importantly, you must take into account the basic reality that you are not an island, split off and alone. If being a good wife and being a good mother is important to you, there will be times when your ability to quickly identify and respond to the feelings of your children and your husband is probably the most single important thing you could do to aid their growth at that time and under those conditions!

Retaining this mental set of reasonable flexibility and openness is not easy. It demands a high degree of objectivity.

Let me draw a parallel. Many mothers have validly said, "I'm able to read my child's cries. There is a whining cry of boredom, a demanding cry for attention, a heightened cry of hurt, an irritated cry for something the infant wants."

What this mother does in response to the cry clearly depends on her ability to "read" it accurately. She does not respond to every cry, nor does she respond in the same way to each cry she hears. Does she *read* the feelings of her preschool children? Does she *read* the difference between a chronic mood and a moment's irritation? Does she *read* her husband's feelings? Does she differentiate between a kind of chronic groping dissatisfaction and a day's end sigh, a moment of crankiness?

Let's assume you are this wife and mother—and let's assume you've become quite astute in "reading" the feelings of key others in your life.

Assume it's now Friday evening. Your husband has been home from work only half an hour. You had made previously an informal contract which would involve his taking the children out for pizza and your continued involvement in a painting. For several weeks the informal contract has been satisfactorily maintained. This particular Friday evening your husband does not seem quite himself. He hasn't complained about the commuter train or the car pool; he seems to have withdrawn into himself. His cheeks are flushed. Clearly he's had a couple or three drinks.

You ask what's wrong. Listlessly he responds, "Nothing."

You read his reaction not as day-end crankiness, but something more important. You could quickly see that the children got washed and dressed in their showsuits, primed and ready for the pizza-bowling junket.

But you hesitate, monitor yourself. You remind yourself of your own mental set of reasonable flexibility. Your husband needs you now!

If you stood tensely at the threshold of the bedroom, paintbrush in hand, and reiterated your question, "I know something's really bugging you, Hank. Tell me what it is," I clearly doubt that he would.

Instead, make haste slowly. Put away the paintbrush. Erase that look of tension and disappointment. Do you really want to respond to his need? Then, create the climate in which this is likely to occur. Close the door. Give him your full attention. Sit down on the bed next to him. Touch him. Try again.

"Hank, I know something's eating you. I can tell. When you feel down, I want to help. Let me in."

"I don't know, Hon. I'm just disgusted with myself. I just seem to be playing out the same old scene—again and again."

What does he want from you? An answer? An analytical resolution to his problem?

No. He wants emotional support, tangible proof that you can accept the way he feels and be sympatico!

"How would it be if I ordered pizza by phone—and we just talked it out?"

He turns and looks at you now, really for the first time today. Something in his expression softens. The problem still exists—but it can be explored now in a different climate. You've related yourself to his feeling, his need. What you've done is what I call *situational linking*.

8. SELF-SUGGESTION—ACTION—
SATISFACTION

Using Reality Control To Achieve
What You Want

An individual wastes time and vital energy. He allows himself to get sucked into trap situations. He gets pressured by events he has failed to picture. He reacts—says and does things—which he regrets. He fails to self-monitor. Now he confronts me with the bottom line result: "I feel so unhappy, so dissatisfied. I don't want to feel like this, but I do. I can't help it!"

I'm sure you see the point clearly. If this individual *does* things that cause him to experience dissatisfaction, how could we realistically expect him at the end of such a day to feel anything but unhappy?

As obvious as this illustration is, it's amazing to me how many people seem to separate in their own minds the things they do from the ways they feel!

Let's face up to the fact right now, if we haven't truly done it before, that feelings are not independent and split-off entities—they are nothing more or less than the *consequences of our actions!*

Thus, if we act in a way that is stupid, we wind up feeling bad. If we do something in a way we regard as being good—intelligent, creative, successful—we wind up feeling happy.

Therefore, what we *do* is the key! Years ago when I engaged in clinical psychological practice with patients, they would sometimes say, "I feel so bad. How can I prevent myself from feeling so unhappy?"

My answer was, "Do things differently!"

Sometimes it took months before the patient could appreciate that I wasn't kidding or teasing him, that I wasn't playing word games, that I had tried to convey a very profound meaning to him, that there was no magic, no insightful interpretation I could give him which would result in his feeling good if, according to his own self-evaluation, the things he had done had been negative! The onus was on him and the key—the road to feeling better—had to be *doing* better!

The Single Biggest Roadblock to Doing Better

But why do you suppose that while thousands of American men and women could rationally agree that doing better precedes feeling better, they fail to perform the very actions they *know* would make them feel happier, more satisfied, more fulfilled?

The single biggest roadblock arises from an unrealistic self-expectation: they set off trying to conquer the whole problem in a single melodramatic action!

Thus, for example, a shy and introverted young woman decides the key to feeling better would be to act like a totally dynamic, extroverted, confident individual—starting tomorrow! The next day she makes a few groping efforts—then wham! She falters and goes to pieces and hastily beats a retreat into her mousy little introverted shell, feeling desperately bad!

The manager who feels over his head and confused by a lot of new technical jargon, research reports and statistics generated by his financial and marketing departments, decides that if he were to become really analytical, a great interpreter of statistical business information, he would surely feel better! That night he takes home the five-year marketing plan, the latest financial studies and projections and various and sundry

157

other systems and electronic data-processing computer reports in his briefcase. He spreads them out on the study table and tries to read and digest them. Things get worse, not better. He's more stupid, less informed, more out of it than he had even dared to realize! Feeling thus overwhelmed, he quits. He feels unhappier than before. Yet, he would tell you and me, "I took action, didn't I? I tried—but it didn't work. See? I feel horrible!" Thus, if you are going to make the action-key to satisfaction work for you—and not have it boomerang or work against you—consider *how* you will put it into practice!

The Key to Big Action Is Little Action!

Little actions, sequenced one after the other, reinforcing each other, build a pattern, a new and successful action pattern—one that leads to real happiness and satisfaction! This is the whole key to translating learning theory into practice.

An adult's learning follows the same principles as a child's learning. Let's take a typical example and see how it works.

Suppose your third-grade child has difficulty spelling. He has a vocabulary list of twenty words he must be able to spell correctly. He feels overwhelmed, discouraged. Suppose you lectured him on the importance of spelling. Would that help? No. Suppose you told him to use the dictionary and sat him down at his desk with it. Would that help? I doubt it. Suppose you sent him to a school psychologist or a private psychiatrist to analyze his feelings. Would that help? No.

But suppose that, without saying a thing to your child, you trotted off to school and worked out an informal contract with his teacher. Suppose you said, "Mr. Teacher, the expectations which you've validly arrived at for most third-graders in your class are unrealistic for my child, Billy, right now! He can't hack them. He's never achieved in spelling! Let's not look for blame. For one month can we agree on a program in which Billy will be required to learn to spell only five new words a week, a hurdle we know he can hack? I'll hold up my end of the bargain and help him every way I can. We'll review his progress at the end of the month, and if he's done well, we can extend the task to eight or ten new words per week." Let's assume the teacher agrees to cooperate. The list of twenty words is broken down into four independent lists, five words on each.

You sit down with Billy and rap about the meanings of these five words. You make sure that he understands what they mean. His assignment for tonight, Monday night, is to learn to spell only one word—the first word—on the list.

This is easy—duck soup! He learns the word, proves to you that he can handle it, fine! But being able to spell the word correctly right now is one thing, being able to remember it and spell it correctly tonight before he goes to sleep and tomorrow morning at breakfast— that's something else! Tell him that after he brushes his teeth and is ready for bed, you'll ask him to spell the word again. Do so. Tomorrow morning the same. He's got it! Success!

He'll probably start spelling the second word before you tell him to. One successful little action leads to another.

Before you know it, Billy will have the five words down pat! He'll feel satisfied, happy. He won't have to be lectured, cajoled, or browbeaten into taking on the second list. To the contrary, he'll probably master it in less than the prescribed one week's time!

Now let's return to the nervous, shy, introverted

young woman. I would ask her, "What things would you like to be able to do differently which, if you did them well, would prove to you that you are less shy?"

Suppose she listed twenty separate behaviors, all of them things she would like to be able to do and which she is not doing now.

On her list is the item *starting a conversation*. She tells me, "I always feel nervous in conversations, especially with strangers, people I don't know. I never initiate a conversation. I always wait for the other person. If he says nothing, neither do I."

I can't help this young woman during the space of one week's time to become a dynamic, extroverted, self-confident creature, nor would I try.

But I *can* help her to act more effectively during one week's time in respect to social conversation. I ask her what kind of things would be fun to talk about with a new girl in the office. Let's suppose she says clothes. She likes clothes, so do most other girls. It's predictable, a presold, pre-established subject of mutual interest. "All right," I say. "Tomorrow morning during the coffee break, I want you to go to the ladies' lounge or the cafeteria—wherever—and sit down next to the new girl. Look her over. See something you like about the way she is dressed. Start the conversation there—with a compliment. Then, as the conversation gets off the ground, if you haven't introduced yourselves, introduce yourself first. Tell her a little about yourself. Tell her that you are interested in clothes—what kind of clothes you like, what kind of buys you look for—and ask her where she got the item you've already complimented her on. Talk with her for only five minutes, but before you go back to your desk, tell her you've enjoyed talking with her and hope that the two of you will be able to chat again."

For those of us for whom such social conversation is

easy, the above example might seem ridiculous. It isn't, however. I've known many a young woman who, without a little positive encouragement, might find doing the kind of thing I've just outlined very difficult, something to avoid.

But what will happen now? The young woman puts the action plan into effect. The new girl brightens up. She enjoys being noticed. As it turns out, she does happen to be quite interested in clothes. She is interested in what our friend tells her about herself. She tells not only where she purchased this particular item, but where she gets most of her clothes. A new relationship is in the making. Our young friend goes home that night feeling good. She *did* differently! She feels differently!

Now let's go back to our discouraged friend, the manager who is overwhelmed by statistical data. Suppose we could ask him what things he wanted to do differently that would prove to him—if he did them—that he was acting as a more analytically competent manager. Again, he could easily generate a list of twenty or thirty such behaviors. We focus on one: analyzing and more effectively utilizing test-market data. What products does he have responsibility for now which are in test markets? Which of these seems to be in the most trouble?

"Clearly, it's Restalgin—so far, it's not getting off the ground!"

What has he done by way of analyzing the problem so far? "Not much," he tells us. He's looked over the early computer printouts and has called a few people in the field. They don't seem to be really turned on, really sold themselves, on the new product. The material that went out from the group product marketing manager was pretty complicated, heavy stuff. He has the idea that some of the district managers in the test-market city may be dragging their heels.

Would he be able to conduct a telephone survey in the next couple of days with each district sales manager in the test-market city and get some down-to-earth feedback on what was happening? If he discovered that the problems had to do with the positioning of the product into the field, could he help to reposition it—even now, while it was in the test market? If he were able to determine key reasons for misunderstanding on the part of wholesalers and brokers, would he be able to get this data with some key suggested action corrections into the hands of the regional sales manager and the marketing support staff?

"Sure, I think so—if I really got on top of this one thing—I'm sure I could do a good job sorting out the problem and coming up with some hard action recommendations that would help!"

We suggest then that he do just this. And he does. He identifies and articulates several key problems that had been previously passed over, unseen. His action recommendations are quickly put into effect. Positive feedback from the field and the marketing department are rapidly forthcoming. He did differently, he feels differently!

Chances are he'll approach the next little action differently. He'll leave the five-year growth plan in his briefcase, he won't try to become a statistical expert overnight. He'll stack the cards in his own favor! He'll parlay a series of little successes into an extended and improved action pattern!

What Will You Do When I'm Not There?

As you've been reading along, you may have felt the impulse to say to me if you were able, "But, Dr. Mok,

162

suppose you hadn't helped this shy and introverted young woman? What if you hadn't been around to help the bogged down manager? What then?"

This is an important question and obviously a realistic one, because when it comes to mounting your own little action plan, I won't physically be there.

But you'll soon discover that it won't matter because you can easily learn to say to yourself exactly what I would say. There's a process which I now suggest for helping you to do it.

Use Self-Suggestion and Be Your Own Reality Control!

From now on, when you consider a major area of your behavior which has previously caused you dissatisfaction, analyze what things you'd like to do differently which would prove to you that you're making progress in this area. Break out one specific action or activity from the list. Have it be a real, down-to-earth challenge, but don't pick the hardest one first. Now the self-suggestion part comes in. Instead of reverting to a self-critical or pessimistic posture and mumbling to yourself, "Oh, this isn't such a big deal, anybody ought to be able to do that thing better," remember, you yourself have gone on record as saying you wanted to handle this type of action more effectively—that you weren't doing well in it up to date. Use self-suggestion to remind yourself it really is important. Use self-suggestion to resell yourself on the importance of doing better at this given type of action and sticking with it until you have proof positive that you've improved. Use this technique to identify some specific ways that you could translate this new little action plan into behavior tomorrow! Use your self-diary to go on record once again in your own mind, to dignify the action, to

163

make it important enough for you to reread and recommit yourself to in the morning!

By breaking down the negative pattern of past behavior into a positive pattern of actions for change and then by addressing yourself to a specific small component of the overall action, you'll now be serving as your own *reality control!* You won't need a private and expensive psychotherapist, or even Dr. Mok, the author of this inexpensive little book, to help you! Because—and I really mean this, check it out with any psychotherapist whom you know—any competent professional would only try to do that which I've suggested, that which you can and will do yourself. Namely, to disallow you from stacking the cards against yourself, to disallow you from trying to turn your whole behavioral pattern around overnight, to disallow you from thinking in global, overall terms, to help you stack the cards in your own favor, to focus in on specifics, to repeat positively reinforcing behavior. That's what we mean when we use the term "reality control."

Many patients in psychotherapy are ineffective in the process we call "reality-testing." This means that they impose upon themselves staggering and unrealistic alternatives so that they must lose or fail. As an objective outsider the psychologist helps the patient to realize that it makes more sense if you don't know how to swim and you feel discouraged about this inability, to splash in the water first, then learn how to tread water, then learn how to float. Then learn how to dog-paddle. Then learn the breast stroke. Then move into swimming.

Beware of Negative Generalization

One of the positive ways we learn and handle difficult situations in constructive ways is called the process of *association*. In time, the brain triggers associations automatically. When we find ourselves in a difficult situation, without conscious effort the process of association quickly furnishes us with a whole host of relevant information, like experiences, significant principles that may bear on the situation, important consequences to consider.

However, what most people do not realize is this: this same process of association can work in reverse, *negatively,* and thus can, if we let it, play a very significant role in hindering us.

Let me give you an example. Suppose a man made a serious financial mistake. No doubt about it. A long time later he is still brooding on his error of judgment, his lack of sufficient planning. "I shouldn't have made that mistake," he begins thinking once again. Almost as though another individual pressed a secret computer button in his brain, he immediately associates with all the details and events surrounding the particular mistake. What happens now is that he re-experiences the pain, the unpleasantness, the frustration exactly as though he were experiencing it for the first time. And not only that! The same association button unconsciously triggers off a whole series of similar mistakes. As though the computer of his brain were now out of control, a gigantic printout of other errors he has also made quickly leap out of the storage retrieval system of his brain: five or six other major errors of judgment, also involving the same principle of impulsivity, of inadequate planning, of overextending himself financially or in other ways, march across the forefront of his mind.

He is mentally beating himself now; the mistakes are smashing into his consciousness, one after the other. *You did this wrong, you did that wrong, don't forget about the other. What was the matter with you; have*

165

you forgotten that you did a very similar thing five years ago?—and not only that, remember the time. . . .

Now he will be unable to sleep. His mind is in tremendous torment. Not only must he vividly re-experience all the pain and self-recrimination associated with this single event he wishes to suppress, a host of other demons turn his mind into a quagmire of incompetence by reminding him of all the frustrations and pains associated with other disastrous events.

As positive experiences tend to associate and form clusters, so do negative experiences. The clusters relate together and form attitudes. Separate attitudes also tend to associate—this is *attitude generalization!*

The man in our illustration has allowed himself to be victimized by the process of negative generalization. The immediate consequences are acute frustration, unremitting pain, pervasive fatigue and depression.

The fatigue, the listlessness and the depression will remain in his consciousness the following morning. It will be virtually impossible for him to get off the ground the next day—at least in an energetic and enthusiastic fashion.

Not only that! Whatever new problem he has to ponder, whatever new decision he has to make will now seem ten times more difficult, the situation will seem virtually insoluble! He will find himself hesitating beyond the bounds of reason. He will not be able to think straight. From the standpoint of action, he will be virtually immobilized. It will be as though a tiny voice within his head were sighing hopelessly, "How can I be sure I won't make the same mistake again? Or perhaps some new and even worse mistake?"

It has often been said that as a man grows older, he becomes more frightened—more cautious, less sure of himself, less confident. Why? Is such a process inevitable?

Certainly not! But why then does the above observation seem so apt in so many cases? The answer oftentimes can be found in the principle of negative generalization! It stands to reason that as a man grows older, the probability for his having made more mistakes than a man half his age is greater, just as the probability for his having done more things successfully or effectively than a younger man is also greater. However, when he begins dwelling on his negative actions, the successes are not also recalled because the process of association, which works on an unconscious basis, mechanistically marshals out all related data and therefore, instead of having to dwell merely on one or two major mistakes, his mind is flooded with fifteen or twenty!

Remember this: you can't stop negative generalization, but you can control it!

Consider the individual whose mind flitted back to his earlier financial error. Recognizing the imminent danger of negative generalization, he would now consciously check himself so that the painful associations need not quicken into consciousness.

One way I have found useful to check such negative generalization, especially if the flow of painful associations is acute, is what I call the *tourniquet technique*.

The parallel to emergency first aid is quite apt. When an individual has an excessive flow of blood from a serious wound, it is necessary to stanch the flow of blood before one can deal with the wound. In this case what you must do is to apply a *mental tourniquet* to the flow of negative associations. This is absolutely essential! Because until you consciously and deliberately turn off the faucet of painful memories, you may not even be able to think in rational terms.

Some people do this quite simply by repeating to themselves, "Stop it! Stop it! I will not flagellate myself to death with the past! It won't do any good! I've gone this route before! I will not take this fork in the road! I know it's a deadend!"

Other individuals whom I've helped to use psycho-energetics have clearly realized that negative generalization represents a gross misexpenditure of vital energy, but are unable to make the *tourniquet technique* strong enough to halt the outpouring of guilt-ridden associations. Several of them found that they were served better at such times by *basic distraction strategy*.

In other words, they sought an ally in their immediate environment which would help them to short-circuit this geyser of negative painful generalization. Thus, some individuals turn to the phonograph and immediately load on a stack of their favorite recordings and turn the volume up high. Choose Beethoven, the Beatles, Jimi Hendrix, Bob Dylan, Scarlatti or Stravinsky—whichever music has strong personal meaning and positive associations for you!

Others change their clothes, put on a sweatshirt and jeans, and run out of the house! For some, sitting in a living room listening to music is not distracting enough! But can you imagine running outdoors at twelve midnight under a full moon, gulping in fresh air, running so hard you force your heart to beat like a kettledrum! Well, some people I've worked with in industry have done it! It works for them!

If neither of the above works for you, *telephone a close and trusted friend!*

This is a very effective technique because once you've related to your friend your momentary but acute feelings of anguish, you can ask him how he feels, what he's doing, what's new and positive in his life. As he responds, you'll find the volume of negative generalization diminishing. Slowly you'll recover perspective. Your friend reassures you. You talk about more harmonious things. You decide to get together for lunch sometime in the next several days. He tells you about a book he's been reading or a television show he's been watching. And gradually you re-enter the world of the here and now.

Another method which I've found works quite well for some people is what I call the *seesaw technique*. When negative painful associations begin pounding into consciousness, try to picture a seesaw. All of the negative, frustrating, guilt-ridden memories have crowded down at the far end, tipping this mental seesaw totally out of balance, to the ground!

In order to regain perspective, you must mount some heavy positives on the other side of this mental seesaw! You can do this in several ways. The first is by forcing yourself to recall a very significant positive thing you've done within the past few months. Something you're proud of, something that wasn't easy. Now, difficult though it may be, reach back into memory, and associate to that!

The more difficult it is to withstand the still unrelenting hurricane of negative associations, the more I would recommend using your self-diary. On a clean page force yourself to draw a seesaw. Head the page, "Positive Associations Only!" Force yourself to write these down specifically, no matter how ridiculous they seem. Usually, friends have told me, by the time they've written down fifteen or sixteen positives, calm and perspective return.

I'll share with you something that I've done to make my own seesaw technique work even better. At the time of this writing, I have no less than seven scrapbooks filled with various and sundry letters of commendation, notes of thanks from various people in industry, feedback sheets associated with various programs I've conducted over the years, notes and letters from various chief executives indicating in very specific terms how the applications of my techniques had measured significant dollar savings in their organizations, and so on. It is a big sugar-candy mountain of pure ego. And if I kept it for no reason but to use for my mental *seesaw technique*, it's been more than worth it!

Thankfully, I've never had to go through all seven books. The farthest I've ever gone is into the middle of the third scrapbook. At that point I laughed out loud! I said to myself, "Hell, Paul, you can't be all bad! You just have an overdeveloped memory! But other people have memories too—and look at the things about you they've remembered!"

Then I went to the bathroom and took a shower, and guess what? I was singing! When I came out, my mind was completely relaxed. The seesaw was pointing in my direction—positively! I was ready for a new challenge right then, my confidence once again restored!

9. RECHARGING YOUR PSYCHIC ENERGY SYSTEM

Wishing and Doing, and the Existential Question Game

The body will deteriorate if regular and physical exercise are not undertaken. In this sense, it is fair to think of the body as an engine and the heart as a battery which needs to be charged constantly so it can more vigorously pump oxygenated blood throughout the entire system.

As a parallel you may consider psychic energy as the oxygen-octane which fuels one's feelings and attitudes (the engine) which contribute to directional movement (behavior). Improved behavorial applications of psychic energy serve to refuel and improve your attitudes and feelings. This, in turn, results in improved behavior.

Admittedly, this is heady brew. But there's an ever-increasing amount of data to support the significance of the above theoretical formulation. In industry, for example, we have hard data based on a population of workers exceeding thirty thousand in a wide normative cross section of job functions (from clerks to vice presidents, from foremen in manufacturing companies to sales managers, accountants, controllers, and so on) which have proved that lackluster performance in conditions which do not permit growth and really meaningful achievement results in marked feelings of frustration, discouragement and unhappiness which are subsequently translated into such maladaptive or unproductive behaviors as absenteeism, lateness, sloppy quality, limited production, on-the-job fatigue, grievances, and so on.

In the late 1940's and throughout the 1950's top corporate managements thought that they could reduce and even eliminate the symptoms just described, by lecturing to employees about company goals, the importance of high production and good quality and by instituting absentee control programs, and the like. These didactic methods, albeit costing hundreds of thousands of dollars, bombed out. In the mid-1960's, largely as a result of research data acquired by Dr. Frederick Herzberg, professor of psychology at the University of Utah, the attention of industry was turned toward the improvement of jobs. By improving the conditions under which an individual is able to work, Dr. Herzberg reasoned, the individual would be able to behave or perform differently in ways that were meaningful to him. As a result, he would feel better about himself. As a consequence of feeling better about himself, he would feel less alienated and would no longer have the need to act in the manner of an angry child, acting out against the unfeeling parental authority (top management) which had previously denied him the opportunity to function as an adult.

What Behaviorial Strategies Can I Use to Recharge My Own Psychic Energy System?

You may be thinking, "Theory in research from industry is all well and good but I'm a housewife—how does this theory apply to me?"

First, let me suggest that many of the things you have already been doing to recycle your lifestyle are examples of how you've been able to rechannel your psychic energy in ways that have probably already proved more meaningful for you. You can build on these. But there are others. Let's explore the conditions under which you are *wishing, aspiring, creating, pursuing goals, growing!*

Are you addressing your attention to the here and now? To today? To the next twenty-four hours of your life? To opportunities within your range of capabilities? Within the framework of reality? If you are, you're ahead of most of your fellow Americans!

Too Often We Fail Because We Reach for the Stars!

If you set a standard for yourself that is totally out of reach, any positive action you take, even if it is an improvement over your actions of last month or last year, will automatically seem to represent a failure when you remind yourself how far below your original lofty standard your behavior really is. Instead of being able to derive comfort and a feeling of positive reinforcement from very valid accomplishment, you'll have to berate yourself because after all your behavior didn't measure up to that in the far-flung dream.

Many people dream themselves into mental breakdowns, alcoholism, depressive immobilization—and sometimes even suicide! Their dreams, albeit well intended and very genuine, become their own destructive whipping masters!

Let's cite a down-to-earth example. A twenty-five-year-old woman is an executive secretary but somehow she feels an inner urge to create, to be and do something more than what she is right now. She is attractive, well groomed and intelligent. She decides to reach for the stars—and soon aspires to become a famous Hollywood actress.

Let's imagine that she takes acting lessons, dancing lessons, exercise classes, and the like. Let's also assume that she answers one hundred and fifty casting calls, but within two years' time has little to show for it except a bruised ego, a lot of hard knocks, painful frustration and a couple of minor credits in remote summer stock. Let's also assume that in the course of her new life she received several opportunities to model at industrial shows, conventions and for a television commercial or two. Let's say she did very well in these latter activities—got very positive feedback, earned above average wages, and was called back for other assignments. Let's even say she registered at a well-known model agency and within a relatively short period of time became a top fashion model.

Now she evaluates where she is, what she's accomplished and how she feels about herself. Obviously she is a failure!

After all, she is not a famous Hollywood actress, is she? She has not landed a major role in a Broadway play. She has not even landed a minor one. She is frustrated, angry and resentful.

Why? Because it's a bad world? Because she's a poor actress? Because casting directors are no damn good? Because there are not enough plays or films being made?

I don't think so. While every one of these factors may have within it its grain of truth, the real reason she feels like a failure is because the benchmark for her own self-evaluation was unrealistically and impulsively arrived at. Her "reaching for the stars" dream may not have been right for her. But this young woman (and so many others in similar situations) questions her own adequacy instead of questioning the appropriateness of her dream!

I have approximately three file cabinets full of data concerning the frustrations and depressions of normal American men and women which are directly related to unrealistic, tortuously difficult, inappropriate but nevertheless self-imposed aspirations.

I'm not suggesting for one single second that we shouldn't dream, that we shouldn't try, but I *will* suggest another way—a less frustrating and depressing one—toward growth and success!

Get Inside Your Own Onion!

This exhortation may strike you as being somewhat odd—perhaps even facetious. It isn't meant to be. A few years ago I reread the play *Peer Gynt* by Henrik Ibsen, in which he compares an individual to an onion, and to his growth as the process of proceeding within himself, layer by layer, translating each inner layer into action until he discovers his own center, his own core which he then tries to use as the focal point for future growth and creativity! I wish I had been able to understand this analogy as a much younger man. As an adolescent I dreamed many dreams. I was at war with many people, and, I suppose because I had a sharp tongue, a number of people said, "Paul, you're good with words—you ought to be a lawyer!"

That sounded good to me. I went and got some books about law from the library, and they were so dull and dreary I couldn't read past the third page. But no matter. Wasn't Clarence Darrow a lawyer? Didn't Abraham Lincoln start that way? And what about Perry Mason? So for some years whenever anybody asked me what I wanted to do or be, I said "An internationally famous trial lawyer"!

Such disgusting arrogance! But worse—I had hitched the wagon of my behavior and my feelings to a star envisioned by people who didn't really know me, a star which was not mine, which had very little relevance in terms of my own inner onion layers.

Years later I did in fact take the law aptitude examination, was told I had done well on it and was admitted to law school. But I never entered. Something inside me didn't feel right. It didn't click. What's more, when I had showed up for the law test, I was one of perhaps a thousand students and I didn't like the way the others looked or acted—one fellow didn't want to remove his coat from the seat next to his, so that I could sit down; another was smoking a pipe and several lighted pieces of tobacco sparked onto my test paper. When I whispered, "Would you mind puffing in the other direction? I've already gotten two spark holes in my paper," he immediately straightened me out. "It's a free country, ain't it?"

Would these be my future professional brothers? There was a negative chemical reaction—call it intuition. I'm sure it was merely a reinforcement of a much stronger and deeper intuitive sense of doubt and about the stars for which I had been reaching all those years.

I walked away after the exam knowing that the results of the test wouldn't matter. This was not the right train for me. It took me many, many years to discover what my real talents are, to find the nature of my "inside onion layers." I am now trying to build outward from there!

Think about it! Are you perhaps taking for granted, turning your back on or repudiating beautiful and original talents you have—simply because they don't fit the template of the "star dream" you imposed upon yourself once upon a time long ago?

To the extent that this may be true, I suggest that you put the star dream on the shelf—suspend it long enough and seriously enough to take a new look at yourself. From within! The things you may discover there could be rare and beautiful, albeit undeveloped.

Get inside your own onion!

So many individuals—particularly men, I've noticed—become so obsessed with reaching the forest of their ambition that they fail to see, much less take delight in, the trees along the way!

How many ambitious, high pressure, aggressive business executives have I known who became old before their time! Who became so obsessed with the treadmill of material success, so caught up in the various corporate political power games and status gambits that they grew farther and farther apart from their wives, from their own children—until it was too late!

They rush through meals, gulp cocktails, fail to exercise, do not avail themselves of musical or theatrical activities, never enjoy the fun of camping with their families, or of making a simple color home movie. They never think of taking their wives for a walk in the moonlight or going cycling with their children in the morning—everything is cut and thrust, thrust and cut, aggressive competition, kill or be killed, be either top dog or an also-ran!

The man who has trapped himself in this process, which I call *ambitious tunnel vision,* will rarely be sought out socially. People will avoid him. He sends out unconscious signals which tell others, "I'm a busy man, leave me alone; don't bother me; I have time and interest for no one but me!" He is investing his psychic energy negatively: in obsessive behavior, in anxiety, in hypertensive worry. He has become the victim of his own psychic energy system, the direction of which he has allowed to slip into the hands of others.

This man needs to renew himself! To get back in touch with good feelings, with experiencing touch, sound, feel, visual beauty: the awakening of his own children, the flexing of his own muscles, the tenderness

177

of his wife, and all the beautiful simple daily knowable things like snow crunching underfoot and ice glistening on trees and the dawn sun rising full and serene against a thousand tree trunks framing the horizon!

This man needs to learn to unwind—not over a vodka martini in a cocktail lounge—but on a country hillside on a quiet evening. He must get to know himself again, peel back the outside onion layers of ambition, dollar signs, stock leverage, living in the future, building economic monuments he will not be able to enjoy, and dig deeper into the onion of himself; to find out what's there and discover a new sense of reality, of wholeness, of fun.

To the extent that *you* are this man or this woman, the first thing I would recommend is taking this Friday off—never mind the excuses, rationalizations or important meetings, the inside of your onion is more important—and take a long weekend with your spouse. Take a couple of good books, your self-diaries or some note paper, some heavy walking shoes and a portable radio.

Don't tell anybody at your office where you will be. Let the whole damn company blow up. Cultivate that attitude—you owe it to the inside of your onion, to your basic self-respect.

It's not actually necessary to take three days in the country to do the things I am going to suggest. You *could* do them at home. However, if you have allowed yourself to race on the treadmill of other people's star dreams too long, a physical shift in scene may help you to symbolize and reinforce the need for a break, a trip within yourself.

Ideally you'll check into a small lodge up in the hills, some place away from the highway and off the beaten track. Decide that tonight for the first time in months you are going to sleep like a baby. You're going to think only about the trees and the land and the country and about feeling good. Once you've prepared for sleep, open the windows wide and let in the fresh air. Breathe deeply!

If it helps you to unwind, turn on the radio and find which plays soft music rarely uninterrupted by commercials. Turn the volume down low. Think about yourself, about what you are, who you are, what you've been doing, whether your lifestyle is one you've slid into, had imposed on you or whether it's one you've consciously chosen, the one you truly want. If you've developed a frantic, outer-directed, up-tight pace, tell yourself it isn't really necessary. You can choose!

Think to yourself, "From this moment forward, I will start thinking differently. I will get back to basics. I will get back in touch with myself. It's not too late. I'm going to live each day starting this minute!"

In the morning stare out of the window and look at the land. Drink in its tranquility! How beautiful it is, how serene. Stare at each thing you see and study it. Don't be in a hurry. Savor the delicate light on each tree limb. Appreciate the fact that you are witnessing a living, growing thing.

Take off your pajamas and walk around in the nude! That's right, it's not silly. Is this something that you would typically do? If not, all the more reason to do it now. Your body is what you are.

Look in the mirror. Try not to be self-conscious. Don't throw back your shoulders and strut around. Be natural. Consider your posture right this second! Are your shoulders slumping? Does your chest feel tight? Have you, like so many others, developed a paunch, a sagging chest, excess tissue in your midsection, waist, stomach, hips, buttocks and thighs? Is this the way you want to look? You don't have to!

Walk back and forth across the room. Straighten

179

your back slowly. Breathe deeply. How does your body *feel?*

How long has it been since you thought about your body? In fact, have you ever done so? Isn't it time you began devoting as much concern to the living structure of what you are as you have to the impersonal corporation's quarterly sales and profit and loss statement?

Do some simple exercises of your choice. Use your secret building block. Remind yourself now, perhaps as never before, of the basic and fundamental benefits involved in recycling your lifestyle!

Shower and dress. No matter how hungry you may feel, discipline yourself this first day to eat lightly. To eat slowly. To give your whole digestive system a break. To get back to the concept of eating only what your body needs and to the concept that eating is an art!

Linger in front of the mirror. Stare at your face. Don't be in a hurry. Take a real inventory!

What do you see in your eyes? Do you see a clear, serene expression? Or a resolute yet flickering expression, a look of tightness? Does your face seem to say, "I'm on guard; in a hurry; tense; overserious; depressed?"

Say good morning to yourself! How did your voice sound? Flat, tired without reason? Where is the bounce, the enthusiasm? Has it died? Did it have to? Of course not. That quality *can* be recaptured! It's within you! It's *your* choice!

Greet yourself again. Greet yourself in the voice tone in which you'd like to be greeted by someone else! That's better. Get a ring into it. Do it several times. With real inflection. Bounce the words out. Make them come buovantlv from down in your chest, not tiredly from the front of vour mouth.

Once your spouse has awakened and is ready to

greet the new day, take a walk before breakfast. Don't be in a hurry. Preferably choose *not* to take a regular road. Instead, walk up a hill so that your feet can feel real earth! Go slowly at first. Comment to one another how the earth feels underfoot, how the land looks, how the early fresh dawn air feels in your nose, mouth and lungs!

Pick up things and look at them. That's right—a gray-black stone veined with chips of silver quartz, a small forked twig, smoothed by time and rain. Feel its curvature with the tip of your finger. Listen to the sounds of the new day. Drink them in slowly. Savor the rustling of the leaves, the fragrance of the earth, the chirping of the birds, the slight whistling of the trees, the almost magical and whimsical whirring of the cricket, the sway and rustle of your own limbs as they move!

Now, increase your tempo. Walk faster, vigorously. Make your body feel it. Walk as fast and hard as you can for about five minutes. Stop! Breathe deeply. Then, just for fun, run in place. Get those knees up high. Swing your arms up and down. Don't stop. Get that heart pounding. Get that fresh oxygen sweeping like a fast current throughout your body. When you begin to feel heady, slightly drunk with the exhilaration and the intensity of the exercise, run in place more slowly. Gradually ease down. Continue to breathe deeply.

Feel the beating of your heart. Not only in your chest. Take your thumb and index finger and place them on either side of your throat—you'll feel the heartbeat in your veins. You're getting back in touch with yourself, with your body, with basics!

Greet the new day! I mean it. Holler out good morning to the hillside, to the trees, to the early morning sun! Listen to the echo! It is as though the earth is

181

greeting you back; a giant seashell resonating with your joy at being alive!

Turn and face your spouse. Study him or her slowly, lingeringly, with love. Study each other this way for five minutes.

Then let one of you tell what he sees in the other one's face. Let this person speak about the features of the other. Slowly. Feature by feature. What do the eyes say? What does the mouth say? What does the hair say? What do the arms and the face say? Now, have that same person touch the other person. Anyplace, any way, the toucher wishes. Kiss the other person's wrist bone, rub the elbows, trace the planes and curves of the body. Follow your feelings. Don't be locked into sterile, mechanical, familiar patterns.

Let the other person do the same. Slowly. Uninterruptedly. Feature by feature. Feeling by feeling. Nonverbal feeling to nonverbal feeling. Touch to feeling. Touch to touch.

Do as you wish. Do as you feel. Hold. Hug. Squeeze. Lift each other up and down. Giggle. Holler. Yelp. Laugh out loud!

Hey, isn't this fun? Isn't it really great being alive, proving it to yourself, feeling it, knowing it, experiencing one's self, experiencing each other, experiencing the new day, experiencing the lemon yellow dawn, experiencing the cricket chirp, creek ripple, meadow lark warble, wood branch, leaf turn and blood beat! Walk back to the lodge hand in hand. Stop. Rub each other. Laugh if you feel like laughing. Sigh, holler, skip, jump up and down. Get out of the old bag, out of the old skin, out of the old locked-in self!

Open yourself to yourself!
Open yourself to the other!

When you go back to the lodge, remember, you're going to eat lightly. If you normally eat bacon and eggs, toast and coffee, for a change order only a pot of tea and some fruit. Drink the tea slowly. Savor its warmth. Enjoy the flavor on your tongue. Talk about it. Touch the fruit before you eat it. Look at it. I mean, really look at it! Take in its form. Its color. Trace the form with your finger. Peel it slowly. With your fingers, not with a knife. If it is an orange, study it. Each section, the fibers, the lines, the way it is made, the way it feels resting in the palm of your hand. Let it roll around. Appreciate, groove on its symmetry!

Let the other person do the same. Don't be in a hurry. Spend half an hour, if you feel like it, getting in touch with that orange!

Crazy? Maybe—but I don't think so. As you get in touch with that orange, you'll get back in touch with yourself, with the way things look, feel, smell, taste! You'll be getting back in touch with nature, with simple things, with growing things. With life!

Each thing you do this day, do it well—and do it slowly. Savor the experience of it. Whether the action be resting, breathing, exercising, looking, touching—do it slowly, do it well, do it thoroughly, do it openly, do it with feeling. Let the inside of your onion come out. Let the buried feelings creep up and surface through layers of self-consciousness, of stultified denial, encrusted worry and fatigue. Begin getting back in touch with *you*, with your own rhythm, with each other!

I would suggest that later in the day you play some feeling games. Silly and childlike though they may seem, they will help you to see yourself, to feel yourself, to get back inside your own onion and out again!

One of these games I call *I'll make believe I am you!* You play it by trying to mimic your spouse. Make your face the way you see and feel his or her face! Make your body posture the way you see and feel his or her body posture. Say some things that he or she

183

usually says, and say them in the same tone of voice. Be a mirror of the other person, but be an objective mirror. Suspend hostility—and defensiveness. The person who is being mimicked should simply try to see and feel and understand what is being mirrored back to him. Reverse roles. Show the other how he or she looks and acts and sounds to you!

Take another walk, later in the day. Take a different route so that you will see and feel and touch and smell different things. Experience the different part of the day differently! Exercise vigorously.

Spend twenty minutes or so getting in touch with a tree. Walk around it, studying it, touching it, feeling its girth. Note the different tactile sensations you experience when you run your hands, for example, over the rough, grainy, course bark of the trunk and down the smooth, slippery, delicate, almost oily bark of a narrow curved limb! Smell the tree and the ground underfoot. Listen to the tree! You will hear a dozen sounds you never heard before!

Walk slowly. Stop and marvel at a hundred small, previously-taken-for-granted things along the way. If you find a flower, don't simply glance at it and hurry along your way. Sit down, one of you on each side of it and talk to it!

I'm absolutely serious. Tell the flower what it means to you. Tell the flower about its petals, about its grace, about its stem. For a few moments try to *be* that flower! Try to mirror back to it, try to reflect its grace! Try to move as a flower would move, slowly, delicately, gracefully, imperceptibly, proudly!

Get up. Bend as a tree limb bends. Move as the leaves move. Dance as the shadows dance.

Go for a run! Feel your own energy! Feel your own organs! Feel your own blood beat!

Stop on a tranquil hillside and play the *hollering*

game! You simply shout out whatever you don't like about yourself. Pour it out, dump it out of your system, spew it out—as much as you can—all the frustration, irritation, fatigue, corporate nonsense, taxation worry, financial anguish, pour it out. Be a volcano. Erupt! Purge yourself! Take turns, each hollering alone. Then do it together! Scream like a couple of maniacs! Use any four-letter word in the book! Don't be shy! That's the trouble—we're all so much more incredibly inhibited than we realize, we've buried so very, very much inside. Release yourself, clear your guts of all the layers of absurdity, of tightness, of pain, of frustrating folly, of inanity, of temper, of impatience, of waiting and delaying and being up-tight!

Later this evening play with one another what I call the *existential question game*. This consists of a dialogue held in the following fashion: The first person asks "What am I?"

The other person responds with the first thing he thinks or feels. For example, "A building."

The first person then may ask, "What kind of building?"

"A brownstone."

"What kind of brownstone?"

"An old and tired brownstone. Stately, but deteriorating. Forlorn. Lonely. But proud. In an abandoned neighborhood. The only brownstone left. Yes, I think a lonely and sad brownstone, perhaps a building that is proud of its past, confused by its present, afraid of its future." The first person can ask other questions about the associator's thoughts about the brownstone or he or she can choose another subject, or a sound, or a color, and ask, "What kind of sound am I?"

The other says the first thing that comes to mind. For example, "The wind."

The first persons asks, "What kind of wind am I?"

185

"A still and almost silent wind, a whining wind . . . creaking in the hollows . . . muted . . . late at night . . . yes, a sad and lonely, cool, late in the night wind . . . the kind that comes before the rain . . . the kind that makes you shiver and worry and not know what the weather will be . . . that makes you think of fire and heavy quilts and protecting yourself . . . a wind that will remain . . . a long and sober, cool and worrisome, long in the dark time, strange and sullen night-time wind." Play the game for an hour with the same person always starting with the question. After the other person has responded with his or her association to the object in the question, the first person can probe as deeply as he or she likes. However the ground rules do not permit the question, "why?" This is done so that the associator is never put on the defensive, never forced to justify his or her impressions and feelings.

After an hour, the roles are reversed. The associator becomes the existential questioner, using any objects the other person wishes as the basis for his or her associations and projections.

The game opens up all kinds of feelings, impressions, associations—data about yourself, about the other person. Layers of your onion will be revealed which you had forgotten, taken for granted, not even realized were there!

The entire three days will seem like a month or two—couples I've encouraged to do this have told me that upon returning they felt "quiet, so relaxed, somehow like children."

But wait! This is not intended to be a split-off experience, a time out of time, ne'er to be repeated. Quite to the contrary! The experience should be a beginning, a platform, a basis for relating to yourself, the other person, your children, your friends—not something to be sealed up and pressed like a beautiful but now dead flower between the pages of a memory book.

You are using psychoenergetics to refresh yourself, to recharge yourself, to galvanize psychic and physical energies previously wasted or dammed up. Don't allow yourself to go backwards now. Go forward. Keep recharging. Stay in touch with yourself and each other!

Remember this: if you feel more, you will have more to give. If you have more to give, you will give more! As you give more of yourself, those around you awaken and respond. They relate to you differently. You will see yourself being involved in more interaction—and at a deeper and more meaningful level.

10. COMMUNICATING MORE EFFECTIVELY—WITH ANYONE!

Effective Openers, Pitfalls and Ploys.

Conversations That Begin Wrong Usually End Wrong

A vital way of improving daily communication is to insure that the climate in which conversations take place is good!

That sounds easy—we take it for granted—but just think for a moment how much energy we all waste every day in unnecessary hassels, in misunderstandings, in arguments that never had to be!

We could have predicted the hassle, the misunderstanding, or the argument ahead of time—simply because the note, the climate, the atmosphere in which the communication began was sour!

Let's look at some common examples. How often when we really have something important to say do we try to rush it? Do we speak to a key person in our lives on the run? Do we stand in his or her doorway nervously waiting for an answer, despite the fact that the topic is serious and that by the very act of standing and hovering we communicate impatience?

How often do we get off on the wrong foot simply because we're interrupting somebody else's activity or trend of thought? Or because we're catching someone when they're off guard or mentally someplace else?

One of the best ways to insure that the conversation will be meaningful—that the other person will really listen and receive your words—is to be careful about choosing a good "start-up" climate!

First of all, if you plan ahead of time to talk to someone about something important, always lay the groundwork!

In other words, convey a few hints—plant a few seeds in his mind about the particular subject and intimate that it is one of special concern to you—that you really respect his or her opinion, that his or her reactions are very important to you, that you don't want to bother him or her now and just skim over the matter lightly, that it's important enough to you and perhaps to him also to get together in a quiet place where you can both unwind and explore the topic in a leisurely way.

In any event, plant the idea in the other person's "mental computer" that this is not just a routine matter. That his thoughts, his involvement are extremely important to you. This way the other person will begin prethinking the topic without necessarily forming a judgment or coming to a conclusion—you prevented this by not alluding to the specific thing you wanted to discuss.

Make sure in advance that you are going to have enough time, that the physical setting is favorable, that you'll be talking to the person in a private place at a quiet time with an absence or a minimum of interruption.

Use Effective Opening Techniques

How many times have we all turned off someone telling us something very serious simply because he rattled on and on as though we had endless time and were absolutely fascinated by every mental detail and intellectual acrobatic trick he could trot out? How many people have turned us off just because they were long-winded! How many people bored us because they wouldn't let us get a word in edgewise, because they really weren't having a conversation *with* us at all but were talking *at* us. Clearly, you can avoid these pitfalls.

Start out a conversation by expressing some sincere interest in the other person. I don't mean reaching into left field for something irrelevant as a means of flattery. But if you notice something positive, or even negative, about the man or woman's expression, play this back in terms of your associated feeling. In other words, if the other person really does look good, let him know. "You really seem rested, relaxed. I haven't seen you look so well for a long time." Undoubtedly he'll be glad to hear it, and he'll probably tell you the reason for his well-being.

But suppose the converse is true. Then say something like, "You seem to be a little tense today. Or maybe tired would be a better word. I hope I'm not catching you at a lousy time. If for any reason I am, it wouldn't upset things as far as I'm concerned to postpone the conversation for a few days."

If the person is acutely upset, he'll probably let you know and will be relieved that you offered him an opportunity for an "out." On the other hand, if he's only been feeling slightly irritated because of excessive morning traffic or the like, the very fact that you identified and responded to his mood will usually cause him to relax, to relate to you as a friendly and empathetic individual.

After the other individual is comfortable, take the verbal initiative. But be brief! Come to the point. Give him a capsule overview—a headline—covering what it is you want; what you can do for him or he for you; why you wanted to see him today. For example: "I think I could really reorganize this whole office in a way that would save us money, time and a lot of emotional firefighting. In order to do it, I would need your backing and complete support. I'd like to explore this further. What's your initial reaction to this objective?"

At that point, stop immediately! Shut up—no matter how hard this may be. Don't try, as so many people in industry normally do, to justify yourself, to bombard the other fellow with facts or details. If you're really interested in his reaction, show that you are by remaining silent. Pay attention to him. Look at him as he speaks. Try to read his response between the lines. Observe him. Does he seem to be holding back? What do his eyes and mouth tell you? What are your nonverbal cues? Are his words positive but his tone sighing, negative? Does he look tired, depressed? Are there other clues that would suggest he is conveying only lip service agreement?

If this is the case, don't rattle on. Don't give him your back-up arguments—not yet. Be prepared to switch gears. Be flexible enough to back-pedal and spend all of your time in this meeting just drawing him out and learning more clearly how he sees the present situation or problem.

Stop Countering Once and Forever!

When anybody says something we don't like or don't want to hear, our typical reaction is to come back with what I call the "Yeah, but" approach.

In other words, we counter. We don't specifically say to the other person, "You're wrong! What you said was stupid! I'm going to prove how superficial your reasoning was." But the words, however diplomatic, convey the same underlying message:

But what you don't understand is . . .
Yeah, but that won't work because. . . .

191

But you have to admit that. . . .

But any person in his right mind has got to be able to see. . . .

Think how you would feel if anybody responded to you, to something you had just said, with any of those phrases! You'd turn the proverbial "deaf ear"!

Just because you disagree doesn't mean you have to advertise it! Bite your tongue, keep your cool. When in doubt, keep silent. Let the person continue. Let him ventilate his thoughts and unwind. You'll frequently find that he'll begin to talk himself out of his previous position. And maybe he'll do it quickly because you haven't thrown any argument roadblocks in his way!

Everybody Likes to Talk, So Let the Other Person Do the Talking!

Practically everybody likes to be on his own soapbox. It's natural because each of us thinks his own ideas are pretty good. More than that, each of us seeks to be understood.

Now imagine a conflict situation—or any conversation that involves a basic or underlying difference of views—in which each person tried like hell to do most of the talking! Wouldn't that be ridiculous?

Well that's exactly what happens in argument situations! One person raises his voice and increases the tempo of his speech. The other individual interrupts, raises *his* voice and increases the tempo of *his* speech. The other individual can't stand it. The decibels go up, the next interruption comes faster and the cruel, judgmental words start flying!

You don't have to fall into this instinctive *adversary trap.* Be patient. Be cool. Make a pact with yourself before the conversation even starts that you will not only let the other person do most of the talking, you'll encourage him or her to do just that!

What a refreshing change you will see! People will like you better, think you're smarter, talk with you longer, and agree with your viewpoints more readily!

Aid Continuity With Simple and Sincere Reinforcement!

I have tape recorded many real-life conversations in industry wherein one individual is trying to influence another in situations such as obtaining approval on a raise or a new budget, hiring another employee, changing the organizational structure or replacing an old typewriter or photo copy machine. Whatever. In most of these conversations, I've noticed that the individual whose approval is needed does not usually trot out his underlying objections or real reservations right away.

Therefore, if it's important to you to get all the cards out on the table, to know what the other person's real feelings or objections are, you've got to make haste slowly. You've got to be patient, hold your tongue and be more quiet than perhaps you'd like to be. Also, it's important to keep the other person coming. In other words, it's important to get him to amplify, to delve in greater depth into some earlier points he has conveyed.

You can do this by using simple, sincere reinforcement! For example, you show your interest in his viewpoint merely by your facial expression. Instead of staring down at your fingernails, give him your full attention. Nod your head. From time to time use any of a number of simple words or phrases which I call *expanders* because they do just that—cause the other person to expand on what he was saying, really feeling or trying to convey!

Thus, for example, if you feel he's only giving you

part of the story, look at him interestedly, nod your head, and say "uh huh."

The other person will typically continue, "What I really mean is. . . ."

In other words, he feels that you're on the same wave-length and is more likely to bring to the surface some of his more delicate points or controversial ideas if he feels the climate is a relaxed and supportive one.

Use the Word-Mirror Technique

An even stronger communication strategy for drawing out the feelings an individual is holding back for any reason is what I call the word-mirror technique.

Try to paraphrase briefly the content or meaning he has just conveyed to you. Remember, I said *paraphrase*. If you come back with his own verbatim words he might mistake you for a myna bird!

However, if you're able to bounce back a succinct paraphrase capsuling the meaning he's been groping for, you've proved to him that you really do understand what he's trying to convey. This is immensely reinforcing!

Another way to do this is not by paraphrasing, but by *analogy!* Suppose, for example, somebody has been telling you about a very harassing job he has been doing. You might respond, "In other words, you've sort of been feeling like a one-armed paperhanger."

In essence, what you've done is to surmise the feeling he had experienced in connection with the incident he had just recounted, put these surmised feelings into a trial balloon and mirrored it back to the person in the form of analogy.

If your surmise was on target, the speaker would probably say something like, "Well, yeah, I certainly did feel that way. I think anybody would. For example

194

. . ." On the other hand, if the speaker felt a different way, had a different feeling associated with the experience in question, he would shoot down the trial balloon. He would deny this as an accurate *reflection* of his feelings, but he would go on to tell you how he did feel. Since this is exactly what you wanted him to do in the first place, you'd be home free! Thus, the speaker might say, "No, you don't understand. It wasn't that way at all. It wasn't that I felt, well you know, frustrated. I was ready to kill the boss! I mean, he really got to me!"

Self-Monitor Yourself With an Audio Cassette!

I mentioned before the importance of a self-monitoring technique! Now you have an excellent additional opportunity to put it to practice.

Why waste vital psychic energy in needless argumentation? Why spin the wheels of energy in pointless misunderstandings when the application of these simple communication techniques can help you to achieve greatly increased rapport with others?

To understand these techniques intellectually is one thing. To use them well, to get into the habit of using them at the right moment, in the right way—that is an art!

Would you like to perfect this art? It's really quite easy. The best way is to use an audio cassette tape recorder. Many people have them, but use them almost exclusively, I have found, for taping favorite pieces of music from records and the radio.

If you do have a recorder, either tape or cassette, make a few recordings of your own conversations with friends or people in your family using the communication techniques I've just described.

Start out in what I call a mini-role-playing situation.

195

If you're married, you might set the stage this way: say to your husband or wife, "I want you to pretend during the next five minutes that I am approaching you in a conversation about our vacation plans this year. For the sake of this experiment, let's assume that what you would like to do is pack the children into the station wagon and drive to Pittsburgh to see your parents. Let's also suppose that I have a very different notion in mind: having one of the college kids in the neighborhood move into our house for two weeks to take care of the children while the two of us take off on our own little archaeological expedition to Mexico. I'll try to set the stage with you, put you at ease, but pretend that I caught you off guard. Try to act as normally and spontaneously as you would in a nonrole play situation and let's see what happens!" Then record the next five minutes of conversation.

If your experiences follow those of other couples to whom I have suggested this technique and from whom I've gotten feedback, I know you'll have a lot of laughs.

As soon as your spouse says, "Why, I'd no more think of leaving the kids with a babysitter than flying in a space capsule to the moon," watch what you say and do.

You'll counter, "What do you mean? That's ridiculous. What's the matter—can't you ever let go of the kids—do you want to molly-coddle them forever? You've got to begin to let go sometime! Why is that so impossible for you?"

Your spouse will then counter, "Stop accusing me of molly-coddling the children. I'm just trying to be loving, understanding, and supportive. Can't you get that through your head?" And so on.

As you play back the five-minute tape of the mini-role play, you'll realize that you very quickly slipped back into the old mode of arguing, countering and energy waste. That's what I meant before when I said the techniques were easy to understand intellectually, but hard to apply smoothly in practice.

Take the same situation again, and mini-role play it from the top. The next time the spouse counters, just nod your head and use an expander such as, "Oh?"

This time around, he or she will say, "Well, what I meant darling, was . . ."

Additional feelings will surface, the climate will improve and perhaps by the third or fourth mini-role play, the two of you will work out a compromise that really makes sense, maybe even one you'd really like to apply this summer!

The reason I suggest taping only five minutes worth of conversation at a time in these initial mini-role plays is that a tremendous amount more actually occurs within a few brief minutes of conversation than most of us have ever realized!

By playing back the five minutes slowly, stopping the recorder to study and self-monitor your tone of voice—the tension, the hostility therein—you'll really pinpoint, diagnose, the ways you typically tend to get off the track, to get farther away from the other person, from his or her feelings and also farther away from understanding.

As you become more patient, more slow-paced, more artful in five minutes, extend the mini-role plays to seven or eight minutes. Then to ten. Always play them back slowly, carefully evaluating what you hear, what you didn't hear that should have come out in the conversation, and so on.

Then, go from mini-role plays to real conversations on points of known difference. If both parties are using these techniques—or trying to develop strength in them—you will have an ideal situation! Not only will you *self*-monitor, but each will monitor the other. You'll have a lot of data to evaluate, but more importantly, you'll strengthen the relationship and the style of interaction with each other!

As this develops, I think it will follow that you'll be building the same techniques with others—people at work, strangers you meet, acquaintances in social settings. People will give you more positive feedback. They'll tell you, "I really enjoyed talking with you. You're so easy on the nerves!"

And you'll feel much better because you'll have less frustration and tension and more vital psychic energy left over to do with exactly as you wish!

PART THREE

PSYCHO-ENERGETICS FOR AN INTEGRATED ACTION PATTERN THAT WORKS FOR YOU!

11. GETTING IT TOGETHER— FOR YOU

Theories and Formulas, Action and Direction

To the extent that it really works for you, that improved lifestyle will stick!

For many years, behavioral scientists seeking to help average men and women gain more satisfaction in their daily lives became bogged down. Evangelical writers groped for formulas which would succeed in motivating people to achieve big and important goals: success, peace of mind, friends, material wealth and recognition. But their didactic and abstract approach didn't work. The reader of these formulas typically encountered difficulty when he sought to translate inspired counsel into meaningful daily action.

Essentially both the behavioral scientists and the purveyors of success motivation short-circuited for the same basic reason: they were trying to develop a motivation tablet which, if only swallowed or believed, would lead to miracles!

In trying to help you recycle your lifestyle, I have tried to approach the problem from the opposite direction. Without relying on intellectual jargon, abstract theory or bold new formulas, I've offered an approach that works if *you* make it work. I've suggested that by applying psychoenergetics, your daily actions will be different. As your behavior shifts in little ways, based on your real inner direction and desire, and you make your psychic and physical energy work for you rather than against you, you'll feel better.

You'll experience a sense of increased mastery, of achievement! And as you experience mastery and achievement on Tuesday, you will be motivated to build on that good feeling and extend the process into Wednesday! By *experiencing* the benefits of psychoenergetic living for several consecutive days—for one week in your life—you will be motivated to build on that success and to experience this type of improved recycled lifestyle the following week!

Your improved, working sequencing of more consistently constructive actions provides the foundation for an increased sense of commitment. And that's what motivation is really all about!

Forget About Theories and Formulas—It's the Action That Counts, Baby!

We have been deceived by many well intentioned and some not so well intentioned authorities and institutions to postpone satisfaction—to exchange meaningful and immediate gratification for vague, uncertain but grandiose futures. In other words, the high school student is conned into relinquishing those studies which might be meaningful in his learning process in order to take up those subjects which will make him increasingly marketable when he seeks college admission. The college student is conned into relinquishing the idea of learning what would be relevant and helpful to him in his daily living on the basis that mastering the curriculum components imposed upon him by the college or university administration will enable him to be increasingly marketable either to graduate schools or to industrial corporations. The corporate employee is conned into the idea that relinquishing his needs for meaningful work and learning experiences right now will enable him to become increasingly eligible for promotion, improved job security, higher-level benefits and future retirement under more favorable conditions down the road! The man or woman who participates in psychoanalytically-based therapy or counseling is conned into believing that he or she should tolerate patiently a lot of intellectual clap-trap because someday, somehow, in the heightened awareness of the future, the alchemy of this process *should* help him to be a bigger, better or more productive guy! The man or woman who attends church on a regular basis has been frequently conned by the clergy into rolling with the punches of life's vicissitudes, cruelties and inequities in the belief or faith that everything is for the best, that all of life's trials will somehow shake out on Judgment Day, that things will be better—even glorious—in heaven or the life hereafter!

Don't exchange your birthright and potential for future satisfaction, growth, meaning and joy or for anything or anybody who asks or requires you to stomach injustice or misery now on the basis of some promised or implied future reward!

As you recycle your lifestyle, remember this: it's the action that counts! Each day, listen to the inside of your onion! Don't think in terms of the vague and far-flung future! The potential for growth, for learning, for happiness exists here and now—today. Don't make deals with others or with yourself. Don't get bogged down about the big picture or the melodramatic breakthrough! Use your physical and psychic energies more constructively, more directedly today! As you do, you'll realize that something beautiful is happening to you! You'll see not only that you are victimized less by outside circumstances, people and pressures which you once regarded as "necessary evils." More importantly, you'll also discover that you are victimized and bogged down infinitely less by your own past patterns of thinking, feeling and acting!

Suppose a man frequently beat his children. If you were to confront him about such behavior, and he said, "I know it isn't very nice, but I can't help it. It's just the way I am, you see," you would have little patience or tolerance for such an explanation! Yet how many of us have responded in essentially the same terms when those closest to us have confronted *us* with our own negative behaviors and actions!

To dispense with our own negative behavior in such a manner is to say, in one form or another, "It's impossible for me to change. It's impossible for me to grow. It's impossible for me to learn. It's impossible for me to alter past habits. It's impossible for me to behave differently!"

You don't believe that, and neither do I!

You can't totally undo twenty, thirty or more years worth of conditioning overnight. But you can and will act differently in one given situation; you can and will live differently on one single day. It is this belief, this unswerving commitment to daily action which is the key to recycling your lifestyle.

Thus, if you feel you've taken your wife for granted, don't try to entirely shape the relationship tomorrow! Act differently toward her for one day! If you've been detached, out of touch with one of your children, don't spend four hours reading books about parent-child relationships, spend those hours doing one fun thing with that youngster which you never did before!

Think of yourself not as a total, locked-in personality, but as an open, walking, breathing, selective behavioral system. Exercise your beautiful opportunities for choice, and growth happens!

Continuously Review and Modify Your Basic Direction—Keep Building on Your Achievements!

I have not yet met the man or woman who applied psychoenergetics in everyday living for three months who failed to find it useful, who did not experience increased daily satisfaction, who did not discover that he felt better and had more time, or who did not cut down his worries or problems to more manageable size!

However, some individuals, notwithstanding the above success, found that they were still experiencing a more than moderate degree of frustration—not with the principles or practices of psychoenergetics—but with the fact that certain major aspects of their realistic circumstances of life remained in the way.

This represents a valid concern and one which you, the reader, may share. Let me cite several common, classic examples:

• A divorced woman with two children and little or no alimony or child support money is living with her mother who cares for the children while she herself works full time in a city office.

• A husband and father has invested ten years of his life in working up to a position of real responsibility in his company, but now that he has achieved it, he is spending more than fifty per cent of his working life on the road—away from his wife and children.

• A widow receiving a bare modicum of income on social security has been forced to live in a rooming house in a dangerous, ugly ghetto area of a large city.

Let us assume that the divorced young mother has conscientiously applied psychoenergetics in her daily living for three months but now says, "So far, so good, but what about my mother? She just doesn't behave properly toward my children. I know it and I've discussed it with her, but I can't get her to change. I'm locked into the situation. Where do I go from here?"

The hard-driving, successful young executive, let's say, has also applied psychoenergetics conscientiously in his pattern of daily living for three months, but now says, "So far so good, but I know that being away from my family more than half of the time is no good. I've discussed it with my boss and others, and while I believe they're sincerely empathetic to my situation, they've been able to come up with nothing except promises for the future and minor token relief along the way. Where do I go from here?"

The widow is enjoying some of the benefits of psychoenergetic living, but now says, "I try not to worry and get bogged down in being afraid, but I can't help it as long as I still live in this horrible ghetto neighborhood! I can't control the crime, the violence, the filth or the noise. Where do I go from here?"

There are no quick and easy formulas or miracle breakthrough answers I can offer these three individuals. The kind of breakthroughs they are seeking are among the hardest one is called upon to make. Let's explore how it can be done.

The Need for Basic Structural Change

There is a fundamental difference between small sequential changes which result in more meaningful behavioral modifications, and a *basic structural change* which provides totally new conditions for improved lifestyle in terms of yourself, the people with whom you relate and an integrated, directed new action pattern!

I cited the above examples of extreme and chronic frustration because in these instances the sequencing of small but nevertheless significant now daily behaviors may not go far enough. They will not perhaps even under the best of circumstances have a significant enough impact on the individuals' basic structure which determines so much of what they do to provide meaningful relief and improvement over the long term.

Each of these individuals therefore must at a certain point come to grips with the possible necessity of a *major restructuring* of his or her life circumstances. It goes without saying that one has to approach the challenge and the possibilities—negative as well as positive—carefully, painstakingly and patiently.

Let's consider the case of the divorced young mother. Suppose, for example, that after a considerable amount of reflection and after long and careful exploration of a number of possible options, she located a job opportunity, not in the city where she now is working, but two hundred miles away, which would involve employment for a lower weekly salary than she now earns, but which would also include a comfortable, university-paid-for apartment for herself and her children as an incentive for her to work as a housemother or dorm counselor at a particular college. Her children, depending on their ages, could attend the university-run day care center or local public schools.

She can't uproot herself overnight. It would represent a major readjustment—cutting herself off now only from her mother, but from a whole network of social alliances, many of which she had found important and satisfying.

For the moment, I'm not suggesting that she *should* make the move; that she *should* move forward toward *basically restructuring* her life along these lines.

Nor am I suggesting that such basic restructuring would be *easy* for her, her mother, her children or others! I am, however, pointing out that for her to recycle her lifestyle in a truly meaningful way over the long term *may* require radical, major action in the form of such basic restructuring!

Consider the dilemma of the successful young executive who has devoted ten years of blood, sweat and tears to his present company but who now deeply questions the value of his present and projected success in terms of the obvious losses of family interaction and experience involved. Let us assume he is correct in his judgment that a major change within his present company framework is not possible; that he would eventually become something of an emotional eunuch were he to remain with the company on the basis of a transfer to a less challenging and dull reassignment to a staff position in the bureaucracy of the company's headquarters, even though such a transfer might provide him with the immediate chance to significantly cut back his presently excessive travel.

Let us assume that the young executive spent several months carefully weighing a variety of options and possibilities and concluded that moving to another company in the same field would not or could not solve the basic underlying dilemma—that heavy travel is an inevitable part of his job function. As a consequence of getting deeper into his own onion, let us imagine that this young man concluded that he could liquidate his expensive home in the suburbs, sell one of his two cars, cash in his vested holdings in the company and have enough capital to purchase a more modest house in a rural area in which he and his family had, for many years, spent their summers, vacations and weekends; that he could trade the recognition, status and fast-track future for a more modest entrepreneurial venture in which he would function as a manufacturer's representative, working in one place, perhaps even out of an office in his new home.

Would it be worth it? Should he do it? I cannot say.

I would not say. But I do say to him and to you that only he can decide! And further, I submit to him and to you that at a certain point an individual facing such a dilemma *must* decide!

Whether such radical action on his part would bear good fruit would take clairvoyance for us to know. I only suggest that under such conditions, it may be necessary for this man to seriously consider the route of basic restructuring!

Consider the widow living on a modicum of social security income in an ugly urban ghetto. The cards of her daily life circumstances are clearly stacked against her! Nothing that you or I could say to her would in any way ameliorate this basic fact, this painful reality!

Let us assume this widow has spent several months seriously inventorying her strengths and talents, her options and possibilities, but has come up with little more than discouragement because she had not worked for many years, her age is against her on the job market, past attempts at interviews with the state employment service, social security officials and others have provided little more than demeaning exercises in futility!

However, in applying psychoenergetics today, on a conscientious basis, she has identified a number of skills, talents, or interests which previously she took for granted, assuming that everyone possessed these particular attributes. For example, let us say she is of a scholarly turn of mind, really enjoys reading and spends quite a bit of her time in libraries. She knows how library systems work but in the past never thought that this knowledge represented a job-related skill, assuming that everyone shared her knowledge. Perhaps she is also very skillful in handicrafts, but again downplayed this particular talent. Suppose that she has always been an excellent cook and still is! And suppose that although she has spent a considerable amount of time doing volunteer work for elderly patients at a hospital in her city, she had thought of this work only as a routine activity which prevented a sense of boredom and vegetation on her own part!

Perhaps this woman, having gained a moderate degree of confidence and optimism through her use of psychoenergetics, has come to suspect that somewhere there may be a hospital, a school, a boutique, a sorority house, a college or other organization which may need her and her particular interests, skills, and talents! Let us say that after much personal research and correspondence, she finally identifies one or two modestly paying opportunities in a far-flung village to become an assistant librarian, a probationary occupational therapist or class teacher, or a cook's helper in a public school cafeteria.

To make such a radical action change will clearly be threatening to her. Not only does she question whether the new situation will work out satisfactorily, she also questions her own stamina, her own ability at this point in her life to hack it. Further, to make such a move would also conceivably involve less proximity to friends, certain enjoyed cultural activities and perhaps also separation from children, grandchildren, nieces and nephews!

Again, I do not suggest that she *should* make such a move. I do not suggest for one instant that it would be easy! Only she can decide! I do, however, suggest once again that a woman under such conditions as I have described will probably find it necessary at a certain point in her life—perhaps in the near future—to make such a decision.

Most of us live under some daily conditions which are admittedly negative, but which may nevertheless not be so acutely frustrating or painful as to require considering *basic restructuring*. However, moderate though the frustration and pain involved in coping with these conditions may be, it is just as important to us that we come to terms effectively with these conditions as it is for the individual experiencing acute frustration and pain to come to grips with those conditions negatively affecting his life! The strategies for dealing with these relatively minor frustrations however, are different. Therefore, with a commitment to psychoenergetics and with a positive attitude, let's explore how you might identify and deal more effectively with those conditions!

12. THE NECESSITY OF CHANGE WITHOUT DAMAGE

Psychoenergetics and the Negative Forces You Face

In many ways conditions involving minor to moderate frustration and pain are more insidious than those which may require radical restructuring! This is because it's so easy for us to rationalize, to say to ourselves, "Well, conditions aren't really *that* bad. I guess I'll ride along just a little while longer." Thus, the individual assumes a *wait and see* position.

When you do wait, *what* do you see? A few months later, or a year or two later, you see that the negative conditions are still negative conditions; that those things which caused you minor to moderate frustration and pain are still causing you frustration and pain!

However, an individual who is seriously applying psychoenergetics to change or enrich his daily experiences would take stock of his situation and identify the negative conditions which were causing him frustration and pain. He would say to himself, "I experienced frustration and pain under those conditions today, and this was wrong. I did, in fact, experience anxiety. I did, in fact, waste time and energy as a result of those specific conditions. Starting immediately I will try to develop an action plan for correcting or improving those conditions and at the earliest practical moment I shall translate my plan into daily action!

212

Common Negative Conditions Which May Be Causing You Frustration and Pain.

The following are some examples of very common negative conditions of everyday living which many of us have come to tolerate, to accept as though they were inevitable. You may recognize some of these as conditions under which you are living right now and which are contributing to frustration and pain. If so, I would suggest strongly that you review them as though with new eyes and proceed in the days and weeks ahead to pinpoint and correct those which represent the most insidious obstacles—from the viewpoints of time, energy and satisfaction—standing between your present lifestyle and that toward which you're aspiring!

• *Three hour's daily commutation to and from work*

For many Americans, travel to and from urban employment centers is taking an increasing amount of time and energy. The process can be fatiguing, worrisome and stressful.

If you are one who long ago habituated himself to the process, saying, "It isn't that bad," but have many times since reluctantly admitted to yourself that it really *is* that bad, perhaps you should consider how necessary and desirable going on this way really is!

If enough individuals such as yourself were sufficiently outspoken in their concerns about transportation improvement, transportation facilities would improve. I would seriously suggest that you re-examine the question of the stressful commutation experience and begin exploring alternatives: organizing a concerted civic action program, or perhaps residential possibilities in communities which, though closer to your chosen place of work, you may have heretofore written off for one reason or another!

• *Spending between one-third to one-half of your monthly income on living quarters*

The high costs of homes and apartments, combined with ever-increasing rates of taxation, maintenance and insurance, are currently forcing millions of Americans to spend between one-third and one-half of their net monthly income on shelter!

This condition is not only negative in and of itself, it sets up a chain reaction of negatives. The fact of unproportionately high shelter expenses leads the breadwinner to invest an inordinate amount of psychic energy in negative and unproductive worry and fear. This investment, in turn, robs him of productive, creative and satisfying experiences. Further, on an economic basis, the unproportionate expenditure on housing frequently causes him to deny himself and his family other basic, positive psychic outlets such as long vacations, three-day weekends in the country, trips to visit close friends and family members in other communities, a night on the town, and so forth.

You are doubtless already aware of the domino-chain of negative conditions caused by the simple fact that you are spending an inordinate amount of money on housing. You must now consider whether such negative conditions are inevitable; whether you should allow yourself to tolerate them as unalterable!

In this area young people are leading the way! They are more flexible, open-minded, experimental and innovative in considering shared approaches to housing which may prove more economical and also more fun! We oldsters (the thirty-and-over generation) are only now beginning to get the message!

We are witnessing an increasing trend toward multiple living arrangements: two compatible families jointly sharing the expenses of a single house; two or three urban families forming an informal communal living ar-

214

rangement in a large duplex apartment; a group of neighbors banding together to acquire—solely for the cost of taxes—a previously-abandoned multiple dwelling and then putting into effect a joint action plan, frequently backed by city support, for property renovation and neighborhood improvement!

Once upon a time such undertakings were often viewed by mainstream Americans as representing the actions of wild-eyed radicals, bohemians, communists, or worse! No more! And perhaps the time has come for *you* to consider the domino-chain of negative conditions created by spending a gigantic hunk of your monthly income on housing! Perhaps it is time for you to reconsider whether such negative conditions are or are not "really that bad"!

• *Self-destructive personal habits*

Many friends and acquaintances of mine smoke forty to fifty cigarettes on a daily basis and consume, on a weekly basis, two quarts or more of liquor. Time and again I have heard them shrug off the negative effects of such behavior with the predictable and common rationalization, "I could stop if I wanted, but I don't really want to. I know I smoke and drink a lot. It's the pressure of modern living. I just can't help it!"

Who are they kidding? Their hearts? Their waistlines? Their mirrors? I don't think so. If they are kidding anyone, it is only themselves.

How about you? Have *you* perhaps been rationalizing these very same self-destructive, negative habits as the consequences of conditions which you could not control?

If so, think for a moment in psychoenergetic terms! Consider how these negative habits rob you of energy and strength, of looking and feeling your best, of feeling fresh, powerful, resilient, youthful!

Think of all the different, new and wonderful things

215

you might be doing if you had more stamina, if you were really fit, if you had energy to spare.

Well, you *don't* have to relinquish such experiences. You *can* exercise choice! Don't smoke or drink today! And as you achieve those first small but significant victories, extend them into tomorrow!

The renewed feeling of energy and well-being will express itself in many ways. You will enjoy the fruit you will eat infinitely more—for the first time in a long while, you will really taste it! You will feel less tired! You'll find you are doing more—things that count, things that you always wanted to do but never felt up to! In time, you will even look better, as you exercise more and as your body receives vitally important increased amounts of oxygen!

● *The refusal to unwind and enjoy*

Millions of Americans are like coiled springs! They are constantly tense and taut. You see the tension in their strained expressions, their stiff body movements. They are up-tight as a matter of course day in and day out. They are chronically griping and complaining. If you confront them with their apparent inability to unwind, they become more up-tight and defensive. "I can't help it. Don't you understand? Its an up-tight world we live in—a world I never made. My circumstances are stressful. There is nothing I can do about it!" These people never seem to relax, to unwind fully. Not only that. You would be hard put to identify any experience, any single daily action which these individuals truly enjoy!

To the extent that your previous lifestyle parallels that of the up-tight people I have just described, ask yourself seriously, "Is this the type of lifestyle I really want? Is it my inevitable destiny to be a coiled spring? Have I perhaps *not allowed* myself to enjoy life?"

I have known some executives in a given fast-paced,

highly competitive corporate environment who were full of bounce and spontaneity, who were able to enjoy and unwind—playing golf two or three times a week, who were able to leave the office problems at the office. However, there were many other executives in the very same company who told me that conditions were too stressful to allow them to relax. They never unwound, they never played golf, they never seemed to have any fun! They put the blame on the company and were frequently shocked to discover that some of their fellow executives, whom they saw as essentially no more intelligent or talented than themselves, were doing the enjoyable things just mentioned!

Remember that in the very beginning of this book I discussed compulsions. Well, perhaps the frantic, do-or-die attitude to your job represents just such a compulsion!

Is the compulsion working for you or against you? How creative will you be in your work tomorrow if you haven't unwound tonight? How strong, understanding and enjoyable a husband or wife will you be any time this week, day or night, or this weekend, if you refuse to unwind? What pleasures will you derive from your life if you allow your compulsion to prevent you from using psychoenergetics for self-renewal?

● *The tolerance for boring, meaningless work*

Repetitive, unchallenging work on a daily basis represents one of the most insidious negative conditions of all! How many millions of Americans are there who spend two or three hours every day of their work lives preparing meaningless reports which no one in their company may ever use and the results of which they themselves never even hear about? How many people are there who, week in and week out, collect data, then painstakingly prepare the weekly widget report—type it, retype it, proofread it and submit up the line—only to have it swallowed up by the huge, nameless bureaucratic vacuum cleaner that represents modern corporate communications? How many millions of Americans have long ago questioned the efficacy of doing such time-wasting, energy-draining, wheel-spinning things, yet have gone right on doing them because "the company requires these reports. I can't help it. I just have to grin and bear it." But do they? Do you? The acceptance of and adherence to the status quo maintains the status quo!

Think of the matter in this light. Let's say an individual averages between two to three hours per day doing unproductive things—unproductive for himself and unproductive for his company! Figuring on the basis of a five-day work week, that individual is investing no less than twelve-and-a-half hours of vital human energy every week in meaningless tasks!

Think what he might be doing instead! How much more meaningful work he might in fact be doing: work that would help his company to reduce costs and show increased bottom-line profits; work that would be stimulating and challenging to the worker himself; work that would involve learning, acquiring new skills, growing!

Imagine what it would be like if he invested those twelve-and-a-half hours per week in learning new computer systems, a foreign language, new inventory methods—even if he spent half of those hours in a company-sponsored physical fitness program!

Admittedly, it's sometimes difficult to buck the system, to reverse meaningless, energy- and time-wasting, institutionalized work practices!

But imagine what it would be like if tomorrow each individual reader of this book chose not to do the daily or weekly widget report, but instead performed an activity that would contribute more meaningfully and directly to the company which employs him! Do you know what would happen?

I'll tell you—because I've gotten other employees and their bosses to follow this selfsame suggestion!

The supervisor of that individual who refused to do the widget report but did something more meaningful and beneficial for the company would smile and sigh with relief. "Thank God you used your head. What you did this morning is much more important than the widget report. Keep it up. Maybe we can send in one of these widget reports on a monthly or quarterly basis instead. Or maybe I can get some of the other department heads to buck it up the line and get rid of the practice altogether. We'll see, but meanwhile keep up the good work and keep using your brain!"

Try it, your company won't blow up and neither will you!

Make your own list of negative conditions and begin correcting them now!

Perhaps the negative condition of daily living which is draining most of your time and energy is something I haven't mentioned: chauffeuring your children to every club meeting, movie or community activity under the sun as though no other alternative existed; spending endless hours once or twice a week at the supermarket as though it were impossible to shop, store food and save money any other way; getting caught up in an excessive number of community, social, civic or club activities to the point of scattering your energy to the winds and then failing to retrench, review your energy investments and plan them anew for fear of rocking the boat or hurting somebody else's feelings!

You be the judge. You decide whether these negative conditions to which you've adapted truly are inevitable! You decide what will happen, what is likely to happen if you merely keep quiet, keep on in the same vein, wait and see.

As You Become More Successful in Recycling Your Lifestyle, Others Will Call You Aggressive or Self-Centered

I don't know of a single individual who has been successful in using psychoenergetics to recycle his lifestyle who has not borne the brunt of some criticism.

Beyond the teasing, skepticism and derisive humor which are typically symptomatic of the jealousy of your friends and acquaintances, I think you will find, as I have, that to many individuals in our society a self-reliant man or woman is very threatening. To the outer-directed observer, such a person is very unnerving! There will be those among your friends and acquaintances who are quick to criticize you and put you down for living in a way that violates their pattern. Don't be surprised if these people label you as aggressive or self-centered—or worse.

What such a person is really saying is, "I'm one of the crowd. I can see that you're not. But you seem to be enjoying what you are doing. You don't seem to need the crowd. I don't get it—that bothers me!"

Because you are using psychoenergetics effectively, you will not feel threatened by his being threatened! You will be able to listen to such criticism compassionately and even with a feeling of reinforced pride in yourself and what you are doing. You'll find that you have energy left to help him if he can be but receptive to your help.

You will experience no need to argue with such doubting Thomases, to defend yourself. You will be your man or woman, be able to draw on your own in-

ner resources and leave the crowd behind. Offer him
your hand and do so sincerely. If he takes it, so much
the better for him. If he does not, figuratively thumb
your nose at him or throw him a kiss! Do a cartwheel
and keep going!

13. RECYCLING AS A POSITIVE WAY OF LIFE

I practice what I preach. Psychoenergetics has personally helped me to grow, to feel better, to do more of the things which are meaningful to me. And the continuous process of recycling my own lifestyle has enabled me to make many new and meaningful friendships and associations through which I have also learned and grown.

I invite you sincerely to be my compatriot, to join in the network of thousands who are using psychoenergetics daily to live, do and feel more meaningfully!

I encourage feedback in the form of letters. I welcome negative feedback as well as positive feedback. If there is anything in this book which does not make sense to you, which you have applied with disappointing results or which perhaps I have not articulated as clearly or as well as might have been desired, I would really appreciate your telling me so in the form of a letter.

If you have used any aspects of psychoenergetics and found that they have really worked for you, I would also appreciate it if you would write me and tell me how, in specific behavioral terms. The acquisition of such data is not only personally and professionally reinforcing, but will also prove helpful in future writings about this subject.

I used to answer all letters from interested readers personally, but several years ago when the amount of incoming mail was such that to answer each individually would have meant an end to my research, study, consulting practice and writing, I started encouraging face-to-face feedback as I go across the nation on my speaking tours.

If you do take several minutes, however, to write us a card or a letter—negative or positive—I will greatly appreciate hearing from you. Write to us as follows:

Paul Mok & Associates
PMA Professional Building
4519 W. Lovers Lane
Dallas, Texas 75209

Thank you!